HITLER'S ESCAPE

REVISED AND EXPANDED EDTION

H.D. BAUMANN

RON T. HANSIG

Hitler's Escape, revised and expanded edition
©H.D. Baumann, 2014

This edition is a combination of two previously published books: *Hitler's Escape* by *Ron T. Hansig*, and Hitler's Fate by H.D. Baumann, including additional information and illustrations.

Published by Piscataqua Press
142 Fleet St., Portsmouth, NH 03801
www.piscataquapress.com

ISBN: 978-1-939739-90-2

Author's website: www.hitlersescape.com

Although the author and publisher have made every effort to ensure that the information in this book was correct at press time, the author and publisher do not assume and hereby disclaim any liability to any party for any loss, damage, or disruption caused by errors or omissions, whether such errors or omissions result from negligence, accident, or any other cause.

Printed in the United States of America

History—an account mostly false, of events mostly unimportant, which are brought about by rulers mostly knaves, and soldiers mostly fools.

- Ambrose Bierce

CONTENTS

INTRODUCTION AND
REFLECTIONS

When writing a book about one of the most despised persons in recent history, one is confronted with two problematic reactions by the reader. The first reaction is one of resentment to hear yet again about this person, or even to hear his name mentioned. Most want closure on this subject and that is quite understandable. The second reaction is one of abhorrence in confronting the idea that what we all learned to be the "historical truth" might not be that at all. Such a revelation can be quite disturbing and unsettling. This is not a book of fiction but an historical account based almost exclusively on, what are purported to be facts published in many history books and other publications dealing with the World War II period and recent Argentine publications. So, let the reader be warned.

At the outset let me explain that I am firmly convinced that Hitler did not commit suicide in the Bunker in April 1945, the evidence is overwhelming (or perhaps I should say, **there is no credible evidence that he died there**.) I am sorry, but I can not accept hearsay as evidence. Incidentally, this view concerning Hitler's escape from Berlin, is shared by Patrick Burnside in his book *El Escape De Hitler,* even though he did not know of Hitler's double and of his means to escape. On the other hand, I have to disappoint my readers by confessing that **I have insufficient evidence to prove Hitler's alleged whereabouts' following his escape from Berlin**. Nevertheless, the apparent fact that established historians have got it wrong, as far as Hitler's

i

demise is concerned, should certainly be newsworthy. This is a scholarly book not meant for entertainment, even though some readers might label it as another piece of "conspiracy theory". Let them, it is their right, even though I would prefer readers who have an open mind.

When considering the fate of the German Dictator, Adolf Hitler, one has to realize that the overwhelming majority of my readers believe that he committed suicide during the last days of the Second World War. This view is supported by dozens of books, written by, among others world-renowned historians. Their views and conclusions are seemingly well supported by circumstances and eyewitness accounts. The mere notion that there may be another, darker side to the story makes us, to say it mildly, emotionally uneasy. Just the thought that such a man, responsible for the death of millions, might have escaped unscathed from the rubble of Berlin in 1945 seems hard to swallow. Yet, as we shall see, there is sufficient evidence in this book, some from recent sources, to at least consider the possibility that Hitler, together with Eva Braun, fled from Berlin on April 22, 1945.

One could easily dismiss such evidence as part of yet another conspiracy theory. But it serves the interests of free people to openly debate even what most would consider being *well-established facts*, despite the emotional problems that this may cause.

There are many unresolved mysteries in human history. One of the more recent ones is the Kennedy assassination on November 22, 1963. Despite all the *well-established facts* surrounding this case, about seventy percent[1] of the U.S. population does not believe that Oswald was the sole killer of the President; neither did a Congressional Committee. For additional information, read Joan Mellen's book *A Farewell to Justice*.

While there is an *official* version of the Kennedy murder, there is also an official story widely accepted, at least by the Western Allies, that Hitler committed suicide on April 30, 1945. This conclusion found in hundreds of books, not to mention in three full length films, is essentially based on a **single report** written in the fall of 1945 by Sir Hugh Trevor-Roper, who had very limited evidence and no corpse of Hitler. Yet, as with the Kennedy story, there remain too many contradictions and unexplained details that cast doubt on the accuracy of this official version. The Russian[2] dictator, Marshal Stalin, who was in a position to know, since his troops occupied Hitler's bunker, told U.S. President Truman and other Western leaders in July 1945 that Hitler had escaped. This clear and unequivocal statement is typically dismissed as "cold war" propaganda. Yet he made these statements only two months after the end of the war against Germany and at the Potsdam Conference, where all three major Western Allies met harmoniously to "divide the spoils" of war. They were still allies in the fight against Japan. The term "cold war" was only coined a year later,[3] in 1946, when tensions between Russia and the West started to build. One of Stalin's successors, Premier Khrushchev, stated in his memoirs: "Stalin naturally insisted for a long time that Hitler was not dead at all..." While we may doubt Stalin's words addressed to the Western leaders, the question still remains: what motives would he have for lying to his own closest advisors and politburo members?

Stalin's statements ought to carry a lot of weight since his troops conquered Berlin and occupied Hitler's bunker. His soldiers were the first eyewitnesses at least to the aftermath of the alleged suicide. Stalin, at that time, had the best espionage service in the world and was said to have a "mole" within Hitler's staff! His judgment as to the events in the Hitler bunker therefore carries more weight than that of his allies, who had to rely on hearsay and on dubious eyewitness accounts. An example of this was Hitler's chauffeur, E. Kempka, the sole key bunker survivor caught by the West. In 1957 he said: "Back in 1945, I told my interrogators anything they wanted to hear." In other words, he lied to Trevor-Roper. Another example is Traudl Junge, one of Hitler's last secretaries. She said in her memoirs that on April 30th she heard a shot from Hitler's rooms. This could not possibly have happened, since she was sitting on the stairs leading to the upper bunker, playing with the Goebbels' children, far removed from the opposite end of the lower bunker and separated by steel doors. The only thing she knew about the "suicide" is what Guensche (Hitler's adjutant and co-conspirator) told her. So much for reliability!

The real question is, why did the Western leaders not follow up on Stalin's lead and request Hitler's extradition from Spain or, wherever he was? I believe the answer lies in the fact that the Allies needed closure on this subject. Only a dead Hitler could bring an end to "Hitlerism" in Germany. Remember, the British and American Governments started the daunting *Umerziehungsprogramm* (re-indoctrination program) for the German people in order to eradicate Nazism. It is probably for this reason that, according to the *Atlanta Constitution* of May 2, 1945: "The British Foreign Office Believes (Hitler's) Death Report." This of course was done without any proof and without an identified corpse. To later publicly request extradition of Hitler from Spain, or Argentina would be to admit that Hitler was still alive. This would not only be an embarrassment for the Western Allies, but possibly might have stirred up a rebellion in Germany.

It is, of course quite possible that Hitler left Spain or, that he traveled by submarine from Europe to Argentina (see

Stalin's statements), as described later. It is well known, that in 1945, Argentina was a haven to quite a few escaping Nazis, Eichmann and Mengele among them.

Recalling newspaper reports about Hitler's escape right after World War Two and after reading several books about the last days of that conflict, my own doubts became stronger and I decided to make a more serious study of the matter, employing a logical approach that a policeman would have while sifting through evidence.

Then again, any author voicing views contrary to established wisdom has to beware – he or she just might be branded a crank or worse.

One may ask, why this morbid interest in one of the most sinister personages of world history? The answer is, that in order to learn from history, we first have to understand it. Let's assume this book was written *pro bono publico*.

Distorted or falsified history may serve a short-term political or propaganda purpose, but in the end it only creates confusion and skepticism by the citizens towards their government.

The aim of this study certainly is not to glorify Hitler, or to make him out as a latter-day hero, but to show him as a coward, escaping justice. History provides ample proof of the incredible death and destruction he caused to the Jews, to Germany and to the rest of Europe and Russia.

There is of course the danger that by exposing his escape, that this may tend to add status to the "Führer" by showing him as "thumbing his nose at his enemies", so to speak. While this may be true, we also have to recognize that more than two generations have passed since this happened and we can also be sure that all participants in these crimes are now dead, forgotten or punished. Finally, there should be some recognition of the fate of the unfortunate Herr Sillip, Hitler's double, who at the end was murdered, as we shall see.

Let's realize too, this is also a great detective story, full of hidden clues, false leads, politically motivated forged evidence, at least one apparent murder victim, and a whole bunch of suspicious characters, braggarts and conspirators.

Like any good detective yarn, we have to look for "motive", "opportunity", and "means", in order to resolve this story. As to motive, we may assume Hitler had a will to survive and a resolve for his body not to become an object of public display and ridicule.[4] He may have anticipated what would happen to Mussolini later on April 29, 1945, whose body was strung upside down from the roof of a garage. These are very strong motives indeed. That Hitler was averse to suicide was testified to by the German Field Marshal, Gerd von Rundstedt, who told reporters after the war, that "...never, never will I believe that he [Hitler] put an end to his own life. That was not in accordance with his nature". The German Grand-Admiral Doenitz stated, "Given my appreciation of his personality, I did not believe a suicide to be possible..." echoing this sentiment. While not a practicing Catholic, Hitler nevertheless had a strong aversion to suicide stemming from his Christian upbringing. It is well known that Hitler disliked organized religions, since they competed against his own ideology. However, this does not prove that he disbelieved in God. Richard Dawkin, in his book *The God Delusion*, made a convincing case that Hitler was no atheist. On the contrary, Hitler invoked God or divine providence in many of his speeches.

As to opportunity, there were still a number of airplanes available on April 22 and 23. The last flight was recorded to have left Berlin as late as April 29, 1945. Also, on April 22, there were still roads open and leading out of Berlin since the city was not surrounded until the afternoon of April 25, 1945.

What was more difficult, as in a "perfect murder", was to leave no trace. Here we come to the means. Hitler had a number of immensely dedicated fanatical followers to help him to disappear. He had plenty of money and still in April 1945, a well-oiled secret police organization. Just to show how much money was left in Germany, it was reported[5] that U.S. troops discovered, in April of 1945, a total of 8,198 gold bars, each weighing 35 lbs. (with a current street value of about $ 5.4 billion) plus 2,474 bags of gold coins, several millions of U.S. dollar banknotes, plus precious stones and other valuables in the Kaiserrode salt mines near Eisenach in Saxony.

Indications are that Hitler and Eva Braun, rather than committing suicide, flew out of Berlin, probably at 8 P.M. on April 22, 1945. What nobody apparently has ascertained, as of this date, is Hitler's ultimate fate.

I, and surely many others, would be eager to find out. There is the possibility that Franco, then the Spanish leader, put the Hitler party into a guarded safe house, at least temporarily, probably in a remote area of the country. Or, that Hitler passed his final years in a pastoral setting in the Argentina's Andes Mountains. However, any lifestyle of enforced idleness in a foreign country must have been unbearable for a person who, in the past, could command millions. On the other hand, the Spanish or the Argentine secret police could have liquidated Hitler quietly, in order to avoid an international embarrassment. In any case, the man is dead, one way or another, and can no longer serve as a rallying point for neo-Nazi elements. That he escaped just punishment for his many crimes is certainly regrettable. Wherever he or Eva Braun traveled, they certainly did so under false names and using false passports. We may therefore never know in which country or how, they finally expired.

At this point one may wonder, why Generalissimo Franco granted permission for Hitler to land in Spain, if this was his true destination.

This involved substantial political risk for Spain. It is true that Franco owed Hitler a great debt. Without German airplanes establishing air supremacy over the Spanish battlefields, the Spanish Civil War might not have ended in Franco's victory. It is also true that Franco refused to join Germany in the war against Great Britain. There were several reasons for this. Spain at that time was an exhausted and devastated country, whose army had neither heavy weapons nor an effective air force. Yet despite this refusal, Franco maintained very friendly relations with Germany throughout the war, which included supply of badly needed raw material and allowing a German spy network to operate on Spanish soil. He even supplied one division of Spanish troops to fight with the Germans against Russia. [6]

Finally there were rumors, that substantial amounts of gold were mysteriously transferred from the Bank of France to Spain a few days before the Allies liberated Paris. Gold and foreign currencies may also have been transported to Argentina, as we shall see later.

Admittedly, piecing the puzzle together is very difficult, not only because of the many conflicting stories by witnesses but also because of the conflicting dates. I admit it would be difficult for me to remember where I was five or ten years ago, or what exactly happened on that day. I therefore relied on dates independently given by several sources or persons. As to the stories of eyewitnesses I again looked for multiple verification; if that was not possible, I tried to apply logic and common sense. A lot of so-called witnesses tend to embellish their tales. An example would be Dr. Schenck, who wandered into the bunker one day before the assumed "suicide of Hitler" and who seems to have styled himself as an expert witness. Yet, his reliability is sometimes questionable. For example, he quotes Ambassador Hewel of telling him that he (Hewel) gave Hitler every morning at 7.30 A.M. a breakfast briefing on foreign affairs. This cannot be true, since Hitler usually got up around noon due to his late night working habits. On the other hand, Hitler's double did wake up early in the morning, the only "Fuehrer" that Schenck observed, if only for a day.

One important clue about Hitler's likely disappearance lies in the differences in his physical appearance, mental health and general demeanor, both before and after his likely escape on April 22, 1945. Many historians failed to consider these distinctions, but it provided me with valuable clues for this investigation. Hitler certainly was very fatigued and tired during the last months of the war. However, this seemed not to have affected his mental and intellectual capabilities up to the time when he left Berlin. As to his physical condition, as the last newsreels and still photos taken on April 20, 1945, attest, he certainly was not a "human wreck", hardly able to shuffle, a description that was applied to the person pretending to be Hitler after April 22, 1945.

Of further interest to the reader may be an article gleaned from the FBI files on Hitler and written by John F. Semsower of the *Central Press* and entitled: "HITLER MYSTERY DEEPENS AS OTHER NAZI LEADERS MAKE PLANS TO LEAVE". This report is typical of the many newspaper stories discussing Hitler's fate during 1946 and 1947.

In this article the question is raised: "Is Hitler dead, or alive and in hiding? If he died, as most of his confederates claim, why then has his body never been found?"

I further quote:

"Allied leaders dislike the prospect of this long drawn-out aftermath of the fall of Hitlerian Germany. Hitler's secretaries have told their captors that he was aware of what a final act of cunning it would be to disappear utterly. So far he has succeeded in doing this better than most things that he attempted in his hectic career.

Many of the world greatest criminologists are on the hunt. They doubt the story of Hitler's chauffeur (Erich Kempka), who contents that he burned the bodies of Hitler and his mistress, Eva Braun, in a shallow trench outside the chancellery. Famed Scotland Yard has pointed out that bodies are not nearly so easily obliterated." And furthermore: "the researchers consider it more than an accident that no remains have been found which can be identified as those of Eva Braun or of Martin Bormann."

When this article was written, in 1946, the author quoted a recent opinion poll which found that two out of three Americans still refused to believe that Hitler is dead.

The author of the article concluded, quite correctly, that to combat such skepticism and the many rumors about Hitler's whereabouts, the Allies were trying very hard to find conclusive proof that Hitler was slain or killed himself in the maelstrom of the fall of Berlin.

My own researches lead me to the conclusion that such *conclusive proof* is still lacking.

This author and many others find it illogical and un-believable that a despicable creature, who caused a World War leading to the death of 60 million people and un-imaginable destruction, should walk away unpunished, yet this seems to be the case.

Here are the main points that made me decide to investigate this matter:

1. Marshal Stalin's insistence that Hitler fled to Spain or Argentina.

2. The numerous newspaper reports between 1945 and 1947 insinuating that Hitler escaped.

3. The fact that the Russians could not produce Hitler's corpse.

3. The statement by SS General Müller that Hitler flew out of Berlin on April 22, 1945.

4. The fact that the Russians found the buried and unburned corpse of Hitler's double close to the bunker.

5. The fact that an x-ray taken from the head of Hitler's double later was used as identification of teeth allegedly belonging to Hitler in order to support the suicide story.

Unfortunately, the late date eliminates all chances of finding eyewitnesses that may still be alive. The real story of what happened went with them to their graves. Even if the eyewitnesses were still alive, their sworn oath to secrecy would make their testimony suspect. Yet there is sufficient new evidence that I discovered, partly in unearthed documentation and in recently published books on the subject, to at least throw serious doubt on the established version of Hitler's death.

It should give us pause when we realize that literally hundreds of books and at least three full lengths movies about Hitler's last days have their roots in the unconvincing report by Trevor-Roper's dated November 1, 1945. This not very thorough report was compiled in only four weeks time.

In addition, there was no corpse of Hitler available, as Trevor-Roper himself conceded. Nevertheless, his story is now accepted history.

While the reader may decide what is true or false in this story, the following writings reflect my own thoughts of what really happened between April 20 and May 2 1945. Additional material deals with his supposed arrival and his residency in Argentina, which admittedly is more circumstantial.

To those readers who say: "This is nothing but a conspiracy theory" I say: "Prove to me that Hitler committed suicide in the bunker, by showing me evidence which stands up in a court of law".

So far, nobody has been able to do so.

Reading this book may be disturbing to some of my readers, since it will challenge a cherished belief, a belief that one wants to hold on to, since it provides a sense of comfort. Yet one should have the courage to at least look at contradictory evidence and evaluate what really might have happened, in order to understand this part of world history.

Notes

[1] From a November 2003 CNN television survey.

[2] I typically use the word "Russian" instead of the former "Soviet", and "Russian Army" for "Red Army", in order to make it easier for the modern reader.

[3] By Herbert Bayard Swope.

4 He expressed this fear many times to his sub--ordinates.

[5]Brown, Anthony Cave, *The Last Hero, Wild Bill Donovan*, Vintage Books, a division of Random House, 1984.

6 Boven, Wayne H. , *Spaniards and Nazi Germany*, University of Missouri Press, 2000, p. 107.

1 | WHO WAS THIS HITLER?

Who was this person, responsible for the death of millions and the destroyer of countries? Was he mentally deranged, as many claim? But if this was true, how come he had so many reasonably intelligent followers? In order to answer some of these questions, I thought it best to make my readers, especially the younger ones, familiar with the historical background, and to provide the setting as it were to the climax of World War Two in the spring of 1945. It is now more than sixty years ago when this cataclysm occurred, and memories do fade. What we learn about Hitler is usually restricted to reruns of old movies about him, or television entertainment masquerading as historical documentation.

History books in themselves do not always provide a clear and unbiased view or reference source either, especially when the subject of the book is publicly despised.

As an example, we are hard pressed to find an objective appraisal of Attila the Hun. Even though he died over 1,500 years ago, his name still sends shudders down our spines; yet few know that he was, for his age, a well-educated man and a good administrator of an empire stretching at one time from the Asian steppes to the center of today's France. Hitler likewise was at times called a monster, or a lunatic. Yet here is Stalin, one of Hitler's bitterest enemies telling his associates in response to a question whether Hitler was mad: "He certainly was not mad; he was a very gifted person. Who else but a gifted man could unite the German people as he did?"[1]

To understand Hitler, one has to understand the recent

history of Germany, since both are intertwined. When World War One ended on November 11, 1918, Germany was a defeated and exhausted nation even though no foreign troops invaded its soil. However, the German Emperor was forced to abdicate and there was a revolution going on. While the revolutionaries were mainly socialist (a group of less radical adherers to Karl Marx's teachings), the trappings were much the same as what happened in 1917 in St. Petersburg, Russia, where soldiers wearing red armbands roamed the streets and where gangs of civilians took over local and state governments. It was only with the help of loyal elements of the army that some order was restored and the so-called Weimar Republic was formed. Economic conditions, partly the results of high war reparations forced upon Germany by the victorious Allies, and later the economic depression of the late 1920s resulted in a very high rate of unemployment. In addition, the 1920s saw hyper inflation reducing the exchange rate from the original 4.20 marks per dollar to 130 million marks per dollar! These conditions created even more unrest and civil strife, which at times bordered on anarchy. It is against this background that Hitler was eventually able to come to power, being democratically elected, in 1933.

Who was this Hitler? He was not even German, being born on April 20, 1889 in Braunau, then part of the Austro-Hungarian Empire. His father was a customs official and rumored to have been the illegitimate son of the Jewish employer of Hitler's grandmother. Hitler disliked his strict father and favored his mother. As a young boy he read a lot, a habit that he retained later on, and which provided him with most of his sometimes encyclopedic but patchy knowledge. He quit high school in 1906 and he spent his time going to theaters and operas in the provincial capital of Linz. He also started to copy romantic paintings. In 1907, when he was eighteen years old, his mother became incurably ill with cancer, and Hitler left home to study to become a painter in Vienna.

Even though his application to the Academy of Art was rejected, due to lack of a high school diploma, he probably taught himself how to paint, since he painted and sold quite a few canvasses, mostly watercolors, primarily depicting buildings and churches. He had a great interest in architecture. Yet he had already read a lot about racial patterns in people (viz. the Eugenics Movement, which was then in scientific vogue) and nationalistic literature, which in part molded his later political outlook.

In 1913 he moved to Munich, perhaps to escape being drafted into the Austrian Army.

When World War One started in 1914, he volunteered and joined the German Army. Here he served as a dispatch runner on the Western Front. He was wounded twice, advanced to Corporal and received the Iron Cross, First and Second Class, for conspicuous bravery.

He learned of the armistice while recuperating in a hospital, having survived a gas attack. This news filled him with bitterness. After discharge he moved to Munich where he worked as a police intelligence agent, infiltrating the different local parties. One of the parties, the German Workers' Party, appealed to him and he joined. He was member number fifty-five, but soon rose to become a member of their executive committee. He then changed the name of the group to: "National Socialist German Workers' Party" (abbreviated in German as NSDAP).

In 1923 he sensed it might be time to march on Berlin and to replace the "Jewish-Marxist Traitors", as he called the government; but first his party attempted to take over the Bavarian State Government. He tried to do this by marching with his followers to the government buildings, and trying to occupy them by force. However this attempt, on November 9, 1923, was blocked by gunfire from police, and several party members were killed or wounded. Hitler was subsequently arrested for treason, was convicted and sentenced to five years imprisonment. While in prison at Landsberg he wrote his book, *Mein Kampf*, in which he espoused his political philosophies.

After his early release in December 1924, he settled in Berchtesgaden to plan the future, deciding for example to forego revolution and instead prepare to gain power through elections. Having already come to public attention, he now met with such important people as Neville Chamberlain of England and Kurt von Schuschnigg, the Premier of Austria. Part of this attention was the search by the Western Powers, especially England, to find within Germany a party that could be powerful enough to block the rise of the Communist Party (which by then was already one of the largest single parties in Germany). In 1919, the Communists had already occupied and run the state of Bavaria, for a few months, till their leader, Reisener, was assassinated by Count Arco Valti, and a volunteer army drove them out. As a result, there was a universal fear (shared by Winston Churchill) that the whole of Germany might be taken over by the Communists who, in turn, then might spread over Western Europe. This is the reason for Hitler's early support, financial and otherwise, by foreign and domestic businessmen and politicians alike. It is revealing that in 1930 even Winston Churchill wrote:

...that authoritarian leaders might be a new and salutary alternative to the weakening, inefficient and increasingly unrepresentative parliamentary systems in many parts of Europe.[1]

While Hitler may have been despised by many in private, his party and his philosophy were considered the lesser of two evils. After all, he would not expropriate private property, or eliminate wage and income differentials, as the Communists promised. His nationalism appealed to the broad middle-class masses, especially after what was considered the unfair treatment of Germany at Versailles. As a result, he rapidly expanded his power base and the support for him and his party.

He was a charismatic speaker, who was not only a master of oratory, but planned his speeches to include emotional punch lines. Later on he had his rallies brilliantly stage-managed. In addition, he had a lot of energy. On one occasion he gave speeches in twenty-one cities within one week! He mesmerized his audience, especially women, some of whom exhibited the near hysteria that we later found with rock band groupies and following the deaths of Eva Peron and Princess Diana. Hitler also appealed to the lower middle classes by promising those jobs, and to the military by telling them he would defy the Treaty of Versailles and build a great army. Finally, he promised leaders of industry to begin a rearmament and construction program if he was elected.

All this effort paid off. While in the Federal elections of 1928 his party only got 7.6% of the seats in the Reichstag (Parliament) compared to a combined total of 40.4% for the Socialists and Communists, he was able to increase his party's seats to 33.1% during the elections in November of 1932. This made him the leader of the largest faction and, after forming an alliance with some smaller conservative parties, gave him a voting majority. As a result he was asked by then President von Hindenburg to form a new Government, with Hitler appointed to the post of Chancellor.

In retrospect, one has to consider the tumultuous times. Six million people were unemployed; there were almost daily street battles between the competing parties, since each of the major parties had their own uniformed paramilitary organizations. For example, the Communists had their "Red Front Fighting Units" while the Nazis had their SA or "Storm Troopers", the Socialists had yet another outfit, and so on. Just to show how severe this street fighting was, it was reported on May 1, 1928 during fighting between the Communist Red Front and the police, that there were thirty-one people killed.[2]

The new Government, taking office on January 30, 1933, and led by Hitler, proved to be very energetic. It restored law and order and in September began the construction of a network of autobahns. These and other large construction projects drove the unemployment down from 6 million to less than 2 million workers in less than six months! In addition, he launched the production of a low-cost radio and later of the famous Volkswagen car. This was, of course, very welcome news to an impoverished population that lost nearly everything during the First World War, then again during the hyperinflation of 1923, and finally during the worldwide depression. As a result of these positive measures Hitler's mandate increased from 33.1% in November 1932 to 45% in March of 1933, just four months later. The majority of the German people gladly accepted the positive achievements and overlooked the shadows and the more sinister side of Hitler's activities.

In his first year in office, he dissolved the Communist Party and had their leaders interned in a newly established concentration camp near Dachau in Bavaria, one of many to follow. Later in 1933 he called for a boycott of Jewish goods and stores, expulsion of Jews from Germany and, during the war, by open persecution and murder of Jews throughout

Europe.

What kind of person was Hitler? He certainly had a brilliant mind, and he was completely ruthless. For example, in 1934, he eliminated the leadership of the SA (Storm Troopers), who tried to create a second Army in Germany and threatened Hitler's support of the armed forces. He admired Stalin for his ruthlessly extermination of all of his opponents. In a rare self-analysis during the last weeks of April 1945, he regretted that he had not been ruthless enough. He also admitted to serious political blunders, such has his alliance with the Italian dictator Mussolini. On the other hand, he was very gentle with children, women and animals but had fits of anger and outrage if he felt betrayed. [3] His personal life was rather Spartan; he was a vegetarian, did not smoke or drink alcohol, but he liked chocolates. During the war he developed a habit of working throughout the early hours of the night and then sleeping till late in the morning on an ordinary army field bed. He was very keen on personal hygiene and would wash his mouth after every meal. According to Traudl Junge, one of his last secretaries, he would always wash his hands, having touched his favorite dog, before greeting a visitor.

The question always comes up, was Hitler a sane person? Here we have the statement of one of his bitterest enemies, the Russian Leader Joseph Stalin who responded to a question posed to him at a victory banquet: Hitler certainly was not insane. On another occasion Stalin remarked; "—Side by side with Hitler we would have been invincible."[5]

Much is made about his sex life, yet it seemed to have been quite normal. As a schoolboy he liked to look at pretty girls, like other boys. In 1925 he fell in love with the seventeen-year-old daughter, Geli, of his half-sister, Angela Raubal, who was then his housekeeper. He installed Geli in his apartment and she took singing and dancing lessons.

Then on September 18, 1931 she committed suicide while Hitler was traveling. He took it very hard. His later and final love affair was with Eva Braun, then an assistant to Heinrich Hoffmann, his photographer. Hitler had a neat personal appearance but had bad teeth, which he tried to hide when he laughed.

Despite having been only a corporal during the First World War, he seemed to have a good understanding of military tactics, at least where land armies where involved. After the war, the German Colonel-General Jodl unashamedly told his interrogators:

"Looking at the whole picture, I am convinced that he was a great military leader. Certainly no historian can say that Hannibal was a poor general just because ultimately Carthage was destroyed. [6]"

As far as foreign policy was concerned, he quite openly pursued the recovery of German territory lost during World War One and the repudiation of the conditions imposed on Germany by the Treaty of Versailles. His first step was, on July 3, 1936, to reoccupy the then de-militarized Rhineland (the German area west of the Rhine and bordering on France). He had already established universal military service on March 16, 1935, and had started to build an air force. He accomplished this despite feeble protests from both England and France, the latter being beset by divisive internal political problems. Both Western allies had neither sufficient forces nor public support for intervention. As a matter of fact, the French General Gamelin, at that time, did not posses one single unit ready for combat[7]

In his preface to the book *HITLER'S GENERALS*, Helmut Heiber said of Hitler:

"Hitler's vision and instinct for operational questions and opportunities can no more be denied than certain positive and, at least in the clear cut situations, successful leadership qualities: steadfastness and forward driving energy. In addition he had an almost phenomenal talent for memorizing technical military literature and for mastering theoretical military and historical information."

Hitler's first attempt to try out his armed forces came in 1936 with the outbreak of the Spanish Civil War. Here Hitler sent in 1936 the first, thinly disguised "volunteers" to Spain. These were mostly air units with warplanes. Italy under Mussolini also sent troops in support of General Franco. The opposition, the Socialist Government, then in power, received substantial support from Russia, under the leadership of Stalin. This civil war lasted till March 28, 1939 and ended in a victory for the conservative forces under General Franco. This war proved to be a trial run for World War Two, which started only six months later.

In March 1938, Hitler overcame the (British Secret Service supported) resistance by the Austrian Government and annexed Austria, albeit with the overwhelming support of the Austrian population.

Hitler's next aim was to recover the Sudetenland (the former German border area that was given by the Allies to the then state of Czechoslovakia). He accomplished this with a treaty on September 29, 1938 between Premier Daladier of France, Mussolini of Italy and Chamberlain of Great Britain. By now the Western allies were openly disturbed, not only by Hitler's flagrant violation of treaties, but also by the size of the German armed forces and the growth of Germany as an economic power. What is now decried as "appeasement" on the part of Chamberlain was in reality a policy of "stalling for time". The later Allies realized quite well that war with Hitler was unavoidable, but war could not be waged at that time (1938) due to insufficient strength on the part of the Allies.[4] It was now that both the British and the French Governments started massive rearmament programs and began to prepare their people for war. For example, there was no support for war in 1938 within the British Commonwealth countries, yet there was that support only a year later, in 1939. [5]

Hitler's intervention in Czechoslovakia was not entirely unopposed within Germany. For example, General Ludwig Beck, the head of the German General Staff, resigned on August 27, 1938 in protest against the planned invasion.

This opportunity for armed intervention opened when Hitler, in 1939, voiced new demands, this time to reincorporate the former German city of Danzig into the Reich and further establish a land corridor between Germany proper and the province of East Prussia, then surrounded by Polish territory. The Polish Government strongly resisted, backed by a military treaty with England. Nevertheless, after making a non-aggression treaty with Russia in August 1939, which included a provision that the Russian supply raw material, which Germany lacked, Hitler ordered his armies to invade Poland on September 1, 1939. This now was the *casus belli* and both France and Britain declared war on Germany on September 3, 1939. World War Two had started.

It is now generally recognized that this war was in reality an extension of the First World War involving basically the same players.

While the German public was understandably quite disturbed about yet another war, the short duration (twenty-one days) of the Polish campaign made it seem acceptable.

During 1940 Hitler secured his shipping routes for

Swedish iron ore by occupying Denmark and Norway, despite the valiant defense of Norway by British troops. This was followed by a lightning strike at France in May 1940. Hitler was acting throughout as supreme military commander planning and organizing each campaign to the last detail. So far, all his gambles had paid off, despite some strenuous objections by his generals. After the defeat of France, he tried to make peace with Britain, which, at that time, was on its knees.[6] He even went so far as to let the British expeditionary forces escape from Dunkirk in France as a gesture of goodwill. [7]

Following Hitler's peace offer there followed a heated debate in the British war cabinet, where the proponents were lead by the Earl of Halifax. However, Winston Churchill, by then Prime Minister, prevailed in rejecting the peace feelers, relying instead on help from the United States. [8]

In May of 1940 Hitler tried another peace feeler with Britain, leading to the botched flight of Rudolf Hess to Scotland, in order to negotiate with the Duke of Hamilton. According to Russian sources, Hitler knew about the flight of Hess who carried with him peace terms[11], approved by Hitler. The details about this flight are still locked up by the British Government.

Hitler then considered an invasion of Britain, but noticed an unusually large concentration of Russian troops at the border of the then Russian occupied part of Poland. In 1939 Poland was also invaded by Russia, which thereafter occupied the eastern portion of Poland. This was then followed up with Russian invasions of Finland and Romania. Hitler surmised that Stalin was planning to attack Germany too,[9] once Germany was occupied with war in the West (that such plans existed had been verified by former members of the Russian General Staff after the war). These observations were followed up by demands for new concessions from the German Government. The Russian Foreign Minister handed these demands over during a visit to Berlin in November of 1940. This posed a dilemma for Hitler. He rejected the Russian demands but decided to gamble again and planned an attack on the assembled Russian Army starting on May 15, 1941, rather than wait to be attacked himself.[12] Unfortunately for him, Mussolini's reckless invasion of Albania and Greece forced him to rescue Italy first, causing him to delay the Russian campaign till June 15, 1941. This, in hindsight, proved a fatal mistake since it did not allow sufficient time to conquer Moscow before the onset of the winter.

Nevertheless, he caught most of the Russian Army in the open near their Western borders without having strong defensive positions (not needed if you plan to attack yourself). As a result, the German Army captured over 2,000,000 Russian prisoners during the first weeks of the campaign. However, the hard winter of 1941, Stalin's appeals to the patriotism of the Russian people, and his relocation of factories to the east of the Ural Mountains, finally turned the tide and at last stopped the German armies. The entry of the U.S. into the war following the Japanese attack on Pearl Harbor in December 1941 then brought badly needed war material into Russia, and the Russian Army went on the offensive. The turning point came in the German defeat at Stalingrad on February 2, 1943, a bitter battle in which Germany lost 252,000 soldiers. Russia had recovered all of their lost territory by 1944 and by the end of that year even reached German territory. Russia received additional help from the U.S. and the British Armies, when they invaded France on June 6, 1944, forcing Hitler to divide his already decimated armies.

Other military setbacks, such as the defeat of the

German Afrika Korps at El-Alamein by the British, led to a retreat from Africa and additional German losses.

The final German offensive in December 1944, commonly known as the "Battle of the Bulge", tried to stem the tide of American troops now entering German territory from the West. This effort too collapsed and the war entered its final phase.

On April 25, 1945 the U.S. Army and the Russian Army met at the Elbe River and cut Germany in two, sealing Germany's fate.

Two Russian armies then breached the last defensive lines of the German Army at the River Oder on April 16, 1945 and the final Battle for Berlin began ending on May 2nd, 1945. Germany officially surrendered on May 8th, 1945.

Notes

[1] Lucas, John, *The Duel*, Ticknor and Fields, Houghton Mifflin Company, 1991

[2] *Chronik Der Deutschen*, Chronik Verlag, Germany, 1983, p. 926 .

[3] Much has been made of his temper-tantrums, yet most of it was play-acting to drive home a point. Fest, Joachim C., *Hitler*, A Harvest Book, Harcourt Inc., 1973.

[4]----Stalin and his court

5 McNeil, R.H., *Stalin: Man and Ruler*, Macmillan Press, London, 1`960, p. 217.

6Lucas, John, *The Duel*, Ticknor and Fields, Houghton Mifflin Company, 1991.

[7] Ibid.

[8] Correlli Barnett, *The Collapse of British Power*, Sutton Publishing Ltd., 1997, p. 591.

9 Lucas, John, *The Duel*, Ticknor & Fields, Houghton Mifflin Company, 1991.

[10] Ibid.

[11] THE HITLER BOOK, The secret dossier prepared for Stalin from the interrogations of Hitler's personal aides, Public Affairs, New York, 2005,p.71.

[12] See also Irving, David, *Hitler's War*, Vol. 1, The Viking Press, New York, 1977.

2 | APRIL 1945:
LAST DAYS IN BERLIN

Let's start with Friday April 20, 1945. In order to follow the trail of the crime, as it were, we have to study what happened in Hitler's bunker during the last days in April. This bunker, located next to the Reich Chancellery, was originally constructed as an air raid shelter. It had two levels; Hitler and his closest staff used the lower level. The rear exit of the lower part of the bunker led into a large garden.

On April 20, 1945, Hitler celebrated his 56th birthday in what was left of the Berlin Reich Chancellery. Here he was still surrounded by most of his closest associates even though the Russian Army was advancing rapidly on Berlin. Yet there were still roads open out of the city. The atmosphere at this party was understandably subdued. Still, champagne and canapés were served; Hitler gave a number of short speeches and, after the reception, reviewed a group of Hitler Youth who were decorated for bravery. German newsreel and press photographers duly recorded this event.[1] Here he was standing or walking, looking quite relaxed and with a smile on his face.

The news from the front was bad. Two Russian armies had achieved a major breakthrough and were marching on to Berlin. Despite the bad news, Hitler was still very much in charge and seemed in full possession of his mental faculties. For example, during his daily military conferences he issued precise and detailed military orders to his commanders. On April 21, Hitler was trying to set up a counteroffensive by elevating General Steiner to the head of an army, and gave him the 4th SS Police Division, the 5th Jaeger Division, and the 25th Panzergrenadier Division.[2] This is quite in contrast to the "Hitler" we shall encounter after April 22.

Here is a list of the more important figures of his court that were present during Hitler's 56th birthday celebration on April 20, 1945 in the New Chancellery in Berlin and who would have been able to recognize any changes in Hitler's personality or appearance after April 22, 1945, the day of Hitler's apparent escape from Berlin and of the subsequent entrance of his "double" into the bunker.

Reichsmarshall Hermann Goering: drove to Bavaria on April 20, 1945, arrived April 23, 1945. The head of the German Air Force; later committed suicide prior to his execution.

Armaments Minister, Albert Speer: left Berlin April 23, 1945 at 3 A.M. for Bad Wilsnack. He was later sentenced to twenty years in prison in Nuremberg.

Minister of Interior, Heinrich Himmler:departed April 22, 1945 for Hohenlychen, he was also the head of police and Security Services. He committed suicide on May 23, 1945.

Minister for Propaganda, Josef Goebbels: committed suicide in Berlin on May 1st, 1945.

Foreign Minister, Joachim von Ribbentrop;: left Berlin on April 22, 1945; he was convicted and executed in October 1946.

Martin Bormann, Hitler's secretary: he was killed trying to escape Berlin on May 2, 1945.

Albert Bormann (brother of Martin Bormann): he flew out of Berlin on April 21, 1945.

Air Force Adjutant of Hitler, Colonel Nikolaus von Bühlow: flew out of Berlin on April 29, 1945.

General E. Christian: left by plane for Bavaria on April 23, 1945.

Dr. T. Morell, Hitler's personal doctor: he departed April 22, 1945, for Berchtesgaden.

General Hans Baur, Hitler's chief pilot: attempted escape from Berlin on May 1, 1945, he was wounded and taken prisoner by the Russians.

Eva Braun, Hitler's mistress and later his wife: assumed to have left with Hitler on April 22, 1945.

Admiral K. von Puttkammer, liaison officer for the Navy: left April 22, 1945 for Berchtesgaden.

Field Marshall Wilhelm Keitel, head of the General Staff,: ordered out of Berlin on April 22, 1945; he signed capitulation of Germany, was executed in 1946.

Colonel-General Alfred Jodel, chief of operations of the Armed *Forces:* he was ordered out of Berlin on April 22, 1945, he was executed in 1946.

General H. Krebs: committed suicide on May 2, 1945.

SS General W. Burgdorf: assumed to have committed suicide on May 2, 1945.

General G. Christian: ordered out by plane on the night of April 23, 1945.

SS General Mohnke: captured by the Russians on May 2, 1945.

SS Lieutenant General H. Fegelein, Hitler's liaison to the SS Army: he left the bunker on April 25, 1945, then disappeared.

Johanna Wolf:[3] left by plane on April 22, 1945 for Berchtesgaden.

Christa Schroeder:[4] left by plane on April 22, 1945 for Berchtesgaden.

Gerda Christian:[5] escaped Berlin to West Germany May 1, 1945.

Gertrud Junge;[6] escaped the bunker on May 1. 1945, was raped and kept by a Russian officer for a year in Berlin.

SS Major O. Guensche, adjutant of Hitler: captured by the Russians on May 2, 1945.

SS General Schaub, Hitler's chief adjutant: ordered out on April 22, 1945 to burn Hitler's papers.

Ambassador W. Hewel, Hitler's liaison to the foreign office: committed suicide on May 2, 1945.

Colonel Dr. W. Stumpfegger, personal physician of Hitler's double: committed suicide May 1, 1945.

Major General J. Rattenhuber, head of Hitler's security (Begleitkommando): wounded and captured by the Russians on May 2, 1945.

SS General H. Müller, head of the GESTAPO (Secret Police): escaped on April 29, 1945 by plane to Switzerland;

Heinz Linge, Hitler's valet: captured by Russians on May 2, 1945.

Erich Kempka, Hitler's chauffeur: escaped out of Berlin. He was captured later by the British.

All in all about 80 staff members left on the evening of April 22, 1945.

As can seen from the above list, only a handful of people remained in the bunker after April 22 – a date that is very important, as we shall learn later – who knew Hitler on a personal basis and who would recognize his voice or mannerisms. This was important in order to avoid the discovery of a double in their midst. These were:

Dr. Goebbels, Martin Bormann, General Krebs, Major Guensche, Linge (Hitler's Valet), SS General Mueller (head of the GESTAPO) and Baur (the chief pilot)., Admiral Voss, General Burgdorf, Erich Kempka, and Colonel von Bühlow.

In addition there were Rattenhuber, the Chief of Hitler's personal bodyguard, Walter Hewel from the foreign office,

SS General Fegelein and the two remaining secretaries, Gertrud Junge and Gerda Christian. It should be noted that out of the above total only ten survived and were captured later.

The only senior officers present at the short, daily military briefings after April 22, 1945, other than General Krebs, were Generals Reimann, Weidling and Mohnke. Neither Weidling nor Reimann knew Hitler very well. These were local commanders, only concerned with the defense of Berlin. The last of the stenographers, Drs Haagen and Herrgesell, also departed on April 22, 1945 after recording the last situation report on that day. There was no more need to take notes, since, after April 22nd, the formal Fuehrer conferences were abolished.[9]

We know that Dr. Goebbels, Hewel and General Krebs committed suicide and that Martin Bormann was killed while trying to escape. This leaves only Rattenhuber, Linge, Baur, Mohnke, Kempka and the two secretaries as potential witnesses to the identity of the person supposed to be Hitler after April 22, 1945. However, Rattenhuber, Baur, Mohnke, Kempka and Linge were very loyal followers, and any secret would have been safe with them. As to the two secretaries, General Müller told his interrogator[7] "that one of them was older and very loyal while the other one was very young and stupid." Hermann Fegelein, Eva Braun's brother-in-law, was a special case. We learn more about him later.

The days of April 21 and 22 saw all kinds of unusual activities within the bunker while the first Russian artillery shells fell on Berlin. This is especially true of Sunday, April 22, 1945, a key date.

At the noon military conference, Hitler became quite upset and finally ordered all to leave, except for Keitel, Jodel, Krebs, and Bormann.[8] According to later reports, at that private meeting Hitler relinquished supreme command of the armed forces and ordered both Keitel and Jodl to leave Berlin immediately for Bavaria and to assume command of what was left of the German forces. The two generals then left Berlin on that day – April 22 – but decided to stay in northern Germany. [10]

It was a momentous decision for Hitler to relinquish command at that time. Why did he not wait? However, it does make sense if he was planning to leave Berlin on that very same day.

Hitler then ordered Schaub, who had a key to Hitler's safe, to burn all papers that were in the safe located in the bunker and then fly to Berchtesgaden to destroy all files at Hitler's mountain retreat. This was done the next day. Hitler also gave Schaub several 100,000 German marks in cash for distribution to Hitler's and Eva Braun's relatives.

In the afternoon he had tea with Eva Braun and two of his secretaries, H. Wolf and C. Schröder. After tea he bid farewell to these two secretaries and ordered them to fly out of Berlin the same evening. [11] He said the situation looked hopeless. Nevertheless, the girls pleaded with him that they wanted to stay. To this Hitler replied, "Ah, if only my generals were as brave as my women." He then stood up and kissed Eva Braun on the lips[12]. One of his remaining secretaries, Ms Christian stated that this was the first time she ever saw Hitler do this. This seemed to be the last time the real Eva Braun was seen in the bunker.

At 5 P.M. Hitler then called Goebbels by telephone, who arrived at about 6 P.M. at the bunker, together with his family and a mysterious female. Albert Speer, his Armament Minister, and his Foreign Minister, Ribbentrop, also came and said their goodbyes. However, Speer decided to stay till early next morning, departing only around 3 A.M. on April 23, the day when everything in the bunker had changed.

Notes

[1] *American Heritage, Pictorial History of World War II*, Heritage Publishing Co.,.Inc., 1966, p. 574.

[2] Ziemke, Earl F., *Stalingrad to Berlin, the German Defeat in the East*, Center of Military History, U.S. Army, Washington, DC, 1968, p. 477.

[3] One of Hitler's secretaries.

[4] Ditto.

[5] Ditto.

[6] Ditto.

[7] Douglas, Gregory, *Gestapo Chief, The 1948 Interrogation of Heinrich Müller*, James Bender Publishing, 1995

[8] O'Donnell, James, P.,*The Bunker*, Da Capo Press, 1978.

9 *HITLER'S GENERALS,* Military Conferences 1942-1945, enigma books, New York, 2003, pp. xxi..

10 *Chronik Der Deutschen,* Cronik Verlag, Germany, 1983, p. 926.

11 Christa Schroeder, *Er war mein Chef*, second edition, George Müller Verlag, Germany, 1985.

12 Baumann, Hans, *The VANISHED LIFE OF EVA BRAUN*, Publish America,Baltimore,2010

3 | PLANNING TO ESCAPE

It happened during one of the last days of March 1945. The cold evening wind was howling and the storm clouds covered the stars. It was one of those evenings where the winter fights a last losing battle against the coming spring.

The garden of the Reich Chancellery was empty, the security flood lights were turned off and the guards kept a discreet distance. Their attention was turned towards their leader Adolf Hitler who took one of his customary evening walks, leaving the bunker with his favorite German shepherd dog "Blondie". The dog enjoying the fresh air was pulling on the leach and seemed impervious to the cold, in contrast to her master, who turned up the collar of his heavy topcoat in order to warm his neck.

This would have been a routine walk for Hitler, enjoying a few minutes of fresh air and escaping the stale and smelly bunker atmosphere; except that time he was accompanied by a familiar figure. It was Police General Heinrich Müller, the head of the dreaded GESTAPO (Secret State Police).

The privacy offered by the garden and by the darkness indicated that this was more than a routine meeting. Their voices were hushed despite the howling wind and distance between the two men and their bodyguards, indicating that something of great importance, something secret, was discussed.

As described in the book *Gestapo Chief*[1], the conversation started with a discussion of the military situation, which even Hitler realized was hopeless, Hitler then asked Müller about how it all should end and he listed as options:

A. Surrender;
B. Go to the mountains and keep on fighting; or,
C. Commit suicide.

Müller strongly suggested to Hitler not to surrender, there was no point to it. Going to the mountains would only prolong the inevitable. This left suicide, but here Hitler had trouble accepting this idea.

He finally asked Müller what he would do in his place. The answer was: try to escape.

This seemed agreeable to Hitler and he mentioned Switzerland as a likely place to go, but Müller talked him out of it fearing that the Swiss might extradite him to the Allies. He suggested Spain instead, and specifically Barcelona. This city had a port, and it would be easy later to smuggle him out on a ship to South America with the help of Müller's local agents.

This plan then was discussed in detail and culminated in the suggestion to have Hitler flown out of Berlin to the South of Germany and from there to Barcelona, using Werner Baumbach, a loyal and much decorated German air force pilot. It certainly would have looked suspicious if Hitler used Hans Bauer, his chief pilot on this occasion (this is exactly what the Russians suspected about him afterwards; see chapter on interrogations).

Müller then indicated that in order for the plan to succeed it was of the utmost importance to have proof that Hitler was dead. Here Hitler mentioned the use of his double—causing both men to laugh.

Müller's proposal was to send all the staff i.e. secretaries, doctors, clerks etc. out of Berlin just after the April 20th celebration of Hitler's birthday.

All the other important people, such as Goering and Ribbentrop ,would be leaving as well. There would only remain relatively unimportant people in the bunker besides Goebbels, who already indicated he intended to commit suicide. If the Russians found the corpse of Goebbels, that would lend an air of credibility to the whole affair.

Returning now to the evening of April 22, Hitler said goodbye to two of his secretaries, his adjutant Albrecht, Admiral von Puttkammer, and Albert Bormann. Between 9 and 10 P.M. nine of the ten planes with all the staff and baggage, had left Berlin and later arrived safely in Salzburg in Austria. However, the tenth plane, with Hitler's important papers and one of his valets on board, crashed en route and burned. This also destroyed parts of Eva Braun's jewelry.

At about 8.15 P.M., SS General Müller observed Hitler accompanied by his favorite shepherd dog, Blondie, leaving the bunker and walking towards the garden. Müller then met and talked to him there. Also present was Linge, Hitler's valet, and Rattenhuber, his security chief. There was nothing unusual about Hitler walking his dog that evening. Security personnel as always restrained the guard dogs and switched off the floodlights. It should be noted that only the lower bunker floor, where Hitler lived, had an emergency exit to the garden. Thus few people would have been able to notice his customary walks outside. Hitler now thanked Müller warmly for all he had done for him and for Germany and he asked Linge to give Müller a leather briefcase containing a large sum of Swiss francs, a personal letter and a medal. Then Hitler departed through the rear exit of the garden. Linge soon returned, he was crying and said, "The Chief is gone. I will never see him again."

As we shall learn later, Eva Braun had already left the bunker earlier that afternoon and probably was waiting for

Hitler to meet her. Traudl Junge, Hitler's stenographer, told in her memoirs that she received Eva Braun's fur coat under the likely assumption that Eva might not need the coat in sunny Spain.

Rattenhuber now too reappeared and said to Müller: "The Chief is gone but now we have a new Chief," meaning Hitler's double. According to Müller, the second "Hitler" then arrived with a similar shepherd dog taken from the kennel (there were two dogs left) and entered the bunker accompanied by Rattenhuber. Prior to entering the bunker on April 22, the double was kept at the hotel Kaiserhof[2] in Berlin, near Müller's office.

The question now is: where did Hitler go that evening?

According to Müller (who after all should know best, having been the organizer of the whole affair) Hitler left the garden by the rear door and flew out of Berlin aboard a Type Fa 223 twin-rotor helicopter for Hoerching airfield near Linz, Austria.[3] Douglas stated that later U.S. troops discovered this machine there. This might not be the true location. A type Fa 223 V51 (Serial Number 233 000) helicopter piloted by Otto Dumke arrived around that time in Ainring near Salzburg, supposedly coming from Rechlin the big German airbase near Berlin. The U.S. Army captured this machine later in Ainring (which is close to Linz-Hoerching). Ainring at that time was the home base of the helicopter Transportation Squadron 40, which owned several type Fa 233 copters.[4] It seems quite possible that this aircraft returned to its home base at Ainring after unloading Hitler in Linz-Hoerching (about seventy miles away). This particular copter had a load capacity of 1320 lbs, a cruising speed of 87 mph and a range of 272 miles (without auxiliary fuel tanks). It should be noted that Germany had helicopters since before the war.[5] As a matter of fact, the famous aviatrix Hanna Reitsch flew one *inside* the Sportspalast in Berlin in 1938. She was also planning to fly by helicopter to Berlin on April 26, together with General Ritter von Greim, but found that the requested copter was unavailable. She used a spotter plane instead. This must have been Hitler's first flight in a helicopter and, no doubt, he would have had "white knuckles". While he had to fly often out of necessity, there were some close calls, mostly weather related. In one recorded case Hitler was visibly frightened. This happened in 1943 when he foolishly allowed Mussolini (who was a pilot) to fly the Fuehrer's plane back to East Prussia. Luckily, or unluckily, as the case may be, the plane landed safely.

According to Müler, Hitler and at least two other passengers then departed from Hoerching in a four engine Ju 290A airplane for Barcelona, on April 26, 1945 at about 8 P.M. It landed there on April 27, 1945. Mueller stated to his U.S. interrogators that he received confirmation that the plane landed safely.[6]

Incidentally, there are photos in the book, *Gestapo Chief*, of both the helicopter and the airplane. The latter is shown with Spanish markings (the German ambassador gave the plane to the Spanish government). In his book Gregory Douglas claimed that Hitler escaped in a Junkers 290 A6 plane, Serial number 0185. Since Müller did not give this information to his interrogators, we must assume that this identification was based on Douglas's own research.[7] However, this conflicts with information given by Sweeting in his book *Hitler's Squadrons*, where he claimed that this particular aircraft was badly damaged beyond repair at the Russian front in May 1944.[8]

However, he stated that there was another JU 290 A-3, Serial Number 0163, Code PI PQ, that was later located at the seaport of Travemunde[9] near Hamburg. These planes, with special fuel tanks, could have a range of up to 4225 miles. It is intriguing, that this is exactly the airport on which Colonel Baumbach landed on April 28, 1945 before he established contact with Admiral Doenitz, Hitler's successor.[10] It is quite likely that Douglas was misinformed and that Colonel Baumbach, who, at the beginning of April, was made commander of Hitler's Flight Command,[11] flew this plane (Ser. No: 0163) with Hitler from Linz-Hoerching to Barcelona on April 26, 1945, as Müller claimed.[12] This plane then landed in Spain on April 27, and after deplaning Hitler and his followers, was flown back to Germany and more specifically, to Travemünde on April 28. The plane later was blown up at this airport on May 3, 1945, prior to the arrival of British troops.[13]

Such an explanation makes sense, since it fills neatly in the time frame between April 21 (the day prior to Hitler's escape from Berlin) and April 28, when Baumbach claimed he flew into Travemünde. The explanation of what happened during these days was left out in Baumbach's memoirs. The reader may guess the reason why. In this regards, it is of interest to note the statements made by Walter Schellenberg, SS Chief Himmler's foreign intelligence chief who stated after the war, that Baumbach was missing and his whereabouts unknown. It was also stated that the German Air Force was unable to trace Baumbach for more than two weeks!

The aircraft shown in the Douglas' book, having Spanish markings, apparently was another A290 plane which arrived on April 5, 1945 on a scheduled flight from Germany and operated by the German airline Lufthansa.[14] Incidentally, this was the last commercial flight from Germany to Spain.[15]

What is less clear was who accompanied Hitler. The original flight order listed, besides Hitler and Eva Braun, Dr.

and Mrs. Goebbels, Bormann, General Müller, General H. Fegelein, Dr. Stumpfegger, Ambassador Hewel, Colonel Betz and General Burgdorf. We now know that at least five of the last eight listed above did not go. However, Müller insisted that Eva Braun and SS General Hermann Fegelein were on the plane. One likely passenger who was not on the original flight order was SS General Dr. Hans Kammler (sometimes called "Hitler's gray eminence") who was practically unknown to the public. Kammler, at that time, was head of all advanced weapons research ranging from four-stage rockets to long range artillery and, most importantly, all aspects of the German effort to build an atomic bomb. General Kammler disappeared without a trace after April 23, 1945 from Prague, which is close to Hoerching airfield. This may have been the result of a long and private meeting with Hitler on April 3, 1945. Incidentally, in his book, Philip Henshall also mentioned the landing of the Ju 290 airplane in Barcelona on April 27, 1945, although he had no idea who the passengers were.[16]

Even more of a mystery is the question of what happened after the plane landed. It is quite feasible that General Franco, the Spanish dictator, did hide Hitler and his entourage as a "thank you" for helping him win the Spanish Civil War between 1936 and 1939. It should be noted that Franco could not have won the civil war without Hitler's military support. This should have made General Franco very grateful indeed. Besides, Franco was an honorable man. There is also a strong possibility that Hitler could have gone by ship to Argentina from Barcelona, a possibility strongly suspected by Stalin. One has to understand that there existed a very efficient organization in Spain and later in Argentina which, according to Uki Goni ferried hundreds of German, Austrian, French, Belgian, Dutch, Slovak and

Croatian war criminals and collaborators to Argentina between 1945 and 1950.[17] A good portion of these criminals had been condemned to death in their home countries.

This rescue organization was originally started by SS Leader Heinrich Himmler's special envoy Carlos Fuldner, who arrived in Madrid, Spain, on March 10, 1945 with plenty of funds. This effort was further supported by the Argentine Head of State, Juan Perón, and by prominent leaders of the Catholic Church. These refugees arrived in Buenos Aires either by airplane from Madrid or by ship from Spain. Additional venues of escape opened up, after 1947, through Italy and Switzerland. With the exception of only two of the war criminals (Eichmann and Priebke) all the exiles enjoyed a life of peace and comfort, mostly under false identities.

It is therefore quite possible that Hitler and his wife could have submerged themselves into such a subculture.

The original flight order listed Colonel Baumbach as the pilot of the plane to Barcelona. Werner Baumbach was a highly decorated German bomber pilot during the war, and during the last months of the war, was the commanding officer of Hitler's personal fleet of airplanes. It is very significant, that on April 21, 1945, the day before Hitler left Berlin, Baumbach requested and received a certificate from the German Air Ministry, signed by a Colonel Wiltner, stating that Baumbach was qualified to work as a civilian pilot and that he could call himself a "Flight Captain".[18] This was no doubt in preparation for piloting civilian airplanes in Spain or South America. As a matter of fact, Baumbach later had a fatal airplane accident in 1953 in Argentina. This brings up the interesting question: did Hitler perhaps travel to Argentina from Barcelona on a German submarine (see the chapter "Mysterious Submarines")?

While SS General H. Müller strongly believed that Hitler

flew to Spain, as he originally suggested to Hitler, it stands to reason, that Hitler choose to stay in a different country without informing Müller, for security reasons. Hitler in those days was very suspicious and trusted nobody. In his book *Broken Swastika*,[19] Baumbach, Hitler's pilot, mentioned that on April 21, 1945 he was in Berlin where he received a letter from Speer. Curiously, the next paragraph was completely out of context and stated: "We had fixed up long-range aircraft and flying boats that could take us anywhere on earth". He then switched the subject to say that he was in northern Germany on April 28 and 29, arriving at the Travemünde airport (near Hamburg). There is no explanation of how he left Berlin, or what he did between April 21 and April 28. It seems quite possible that he flew back to Germany from Barcelona on the 27 or 28 of April, after having left the Hitler party in Spain. This seems logically, since a plane left in Spain would have aroused suspicion. Another fact supporting the thesis that Baumbach flew Hitler, is that Baumbach, while in Berlin on April 21, relinquished his command of the Government Squadron KG200 to a Major von Hernier.[20] This freed him from his daily duties and left time to fly the Hitler party to Spain, or perhaps to a German submarine base.

It should be noted here that Hitler's plane has not been the only one going to Spain. On May 8, 1945, Albert Speer's private "Condor" plane flew from Oslo, Norway to near San Sebastian, Spain, with the escaping Colonel Leon Degrelle, the leader of the Belgian SS volunteers, who fought the Russians[21] during the Second World War.

One other intriguing, but less likely, possibility is that Hitler's helicopter flew to the west of Berlin instead to Austria. An indication of this is in a news item of the *Washington Daily News*, dated December 18th, 1947, reporting on the war crime trial in Poland of a German Air

Force officer named Ernst Baumgart, under the headline: "A Nazi pilot flew Hitler and Eva to Denmark". As the story goes, Baumgart apparently testified that Hitler landed in April in Magdeburg (about sixty-five miles west of Berlin) and that Hitler and his wife Eva departed on April 29th, 1945 via airplane for Denmark. There could be some truth to this since the German submarine base at Kristiansand, where some submarines departed for Argentina at the end of the war, was located just seventy-five miles north of the coast of Denmark. On the other hand, this could have been another false clue to throw the hunters off the trail, in as much as Mageburg was already occupied by the U.S. Army.

The next day after Hitler's departure, Monday, April 23rd, 1945, saw many changes. Most of the staff was gone, there was less security, discipline was relaxed and, most of all, instead of an energetic "Fuehrer", there was a feeble, sickly, drugged, and ignorant substitute who had to be kept isolated and who had to be coached on what to say by Goebbels and Bormann.

Here is a statement from Captain Helmut Beermann of the Security Detail that gives some insights of what the situation was on April 23rd following Hitler's departure:

We veterans of the bunker called this day Blue Monday because, with the departure of half of our comrades and the arrival of the whole Goebbels family and Eva Braun, everyone could now read the writing on the wall. The last act was about to begin. My own dream of again seeing Berchtesgaden vanished. Colonel Schaedle, my commanding officer, insisted I stay, since I was by now an old hand in the outfit. Previously, I had enough officers and men to be able to work out shifts, twelve hours on, twelve hours off. Now, every person was assigned to his task for the duration, which might be for two days or for two weeks. I issued sleeping bags, so that some of my key men could sleep at or near their stations. The old spit-and-polish discipline was all shot to hell. Many soldiers were not even saluting anymore.[21]

There are two interesting items in this statement, first there is the arrival of Eva Braun. This must have been a "new" one (perhaps a double), since the real Eva Braun had lived within the bunker already since April 15, 1945, after leaving her apartment at the Chancellery. Secondly, we note here the beginning of a breakdown of morale and discipline. Did the soldiers know about Hitler's departure? Even if they knew nothing specific, then rumors certainly must have abounded.

The significance of the date of escape, April 22, 1945, also lies in the fact that on this date were held the last fully, and steno graphed, Fuehrer Conferences with Hitler's General Staff.[23] This date also marks the end of his regular Conferences with his Navy staff.[24]

The question is often asked: Why was Dr. Goebbels not included in the escape attempt? After all he was already listed in the original flight manifest (to Barcelona). The answer is: As stated above, he refused, despite Hitler's begging. The reason might be a concern for his children. Perhaps a stronger motive was his loyalty of him and that of his wife's toward Hitler. He might have felt there was a need to guide Hitler's double inside the bunker in order to make sure that the charade worked to convince the world that Hitler committed suicide, as planned.

The type of Helicopter allegedly used by Hitler to fly
out of Berlin

A Junkers Ju290, a plane allegedly used by Hitler to fly on 26 April
1945 from Linz to Barcelona, Spain.

Notes

[1] Douglas, Gregory, *Gestapo Chief, The 1948 Interrogation of Heinrich Müller*, James Bender Publishing, 1995.

[2] This probably was the origin of Chief Pilot Bauer's later statement to the Russians about the rumor of a "porter" at the Kaiserhof having great similarity to Hitler.

[3] Hoerching is now the municipal airport of the city of Linz in Austria.

[4] Coates, Steve, *Helicopters of The Third Reich*, Ian Allan Publishing Ltd.

[5] Winters, Jeffry, *Served Straight Up,* Supplement to *Mechanical Engineering Magazine* (100 years of flight), ASME, December 2003, p. 20.

[6] Douglas, Gregory, *Gestapo Chief, The 1948 Interrogation of Heinrich Mueller*, James Bender Publishing, 1995.

[7] Ibid.

[8] Sweeting, C. G., *Hitler's Squadron, The Fuehrer's Personal Aircraft and Transport Unit, 1933–1945*, Brassey's Inc., 2001.

[9] Heiber, Helmut, *HITLER'S GENERALS, Military Conferences 1942-1945,* ernigma books, New York, 2003, p xxi.

[10] Baumbach, Werner, *Broken Swastika*, Dorset Press, 1992, p. 193.

[11] Sweeting, C. G., *Hitler's Squadron, The Fuehrer's Personal Aircraft and Transport Unit, 1933–1945*, Brassey's Inc., 2001

[12] Douglas, Gregory, *Gestapo Chief, The 1948 Interrogation of Heinrich Mueller*, James Bender Publishing, 1995.

[13] Sweeting, C. G., *Hitler's Squadron, The Fuehrer's Personal Aircraft and Transport Unit, 1933–1945*, Brassey's Inc., 2001.

[14] Lufthansa Airlines operated three type *Ju 290* aircraft.

[15] Sweeting, C. G., *Hitler's Squadron*, The Fuehrer's Personal Aircraft and Transport Unit, 1933–1945, Brassey's Inc., 2001.

[16] Henshall, Philip, *The Nuclear Axis, Germany, Japan and the Atomic Bomb Race*, Sutton Publishing Limited, 2000.

[17] Goni, Uki, *The Real Odessa*, Granta Books, London, 2002.

[18] Hermann Historica, 45th Auction Catalog for October 17–18, 2003, pp. 346–341, "Oberst Baumbach Memorabilia"

[19] Baumbach, Werner, *Broken Swastika*, Dorset Press, 1992.

[20] Lucas, James, *Kommandos*, Cassell & Co. 1985, p 200.

[21] O'Donnel, James,P., *The bunkers*, Da Capo Press, . 1978, p. 118.

[22] Joachimsthaler, Anton, *The Last Days Of Hitler*, Cassell & Co. London, 1995.

[23] Heiber, Helmut, *Hitler's Generals, Military Conferences 1942-1945*. ENIGMA BOOKS, NY. 2003.

[24] *Fuehrer Conferences on Naval Affairs, 1939-1945,*.Chatham Publishing, London, 1990.

4 | A NEW "HITLER"

Let's now discuss the person left in the bunker on the evening of April 22, pretending to the "Fuehrer", in order to cover up Hitler's escape and to play his part in what truly was an amazing charade. I am talking about Hitler's double.

The only information I have found on this subject is from SS General Müller[1] and this may not be exact. However, we know from the Russian autopsy of the body of the "double" and from the Nordon Report[2] that the major parts of Müller's description can be confirmed. Finally, there is the well-publicized photo of the "double" taken by the Russians on May 2, 1945,after his corpse was discovered buried in the bunker garden. This photo was used later by the Russians, in the 1960s, to prove that the real Hitler was dead.

SS General Müller stated[3] that he found this man in 1941 and that he was born to the Sillip family in the Waldviertel district of Austria. He was a distant relative of Hitler and worked in Breslau, was a party member, a member of the SA and was unmarried. While he was not "brilliant", he was quite easy to work with. The resemblance to Hitler was remarkable but he was too short. According to an unconfirmed statement attributed to Eva Braun, he was 5 cm (2") shorter (see also the Russian findings, as shown in the Nordon report).[4] The next problem was his ears. These did not match Hitler's, but there was nothing that could be done about this. He also smoked. When he stopped smoking, he gained weight so he had to be put on a diet. The next problem was his accent, which had to be resolved, together with the problem of his height. Here special soles were put on his boots. He learned to use Hitler's favorite phrases when he talked, and was taught his mannerisms. For example, when Hitler laughed, he had a habit of holding his hand across his mouth so his bad teeth would not show. The double had met Hitler twice in order to study him close up. Hitler later remarked that when he saw the double, he felt as if he was looking into a mirror. Joachimsthaler tried to show proof that there was no double by quoting one of Hitler's secretaries, Johanna Wolf, that "...the Fuehrer would never have tolerated this.".This statement is probably true when viewed in the right context. Hitler certainly would have rejected a double being *in his presence*, but not when he would be at a different location. However, in the same book[5] we read about a statement by former SS guard,Hans Hofbeck,indicating that Chief Pilot Baur told him in a Russian prison, "that a man from Breslau had been presented who looked very much like Hitler".

According to Müller the double was used only a few times before primarely after the 20, 1944, assassination attempt on Hitler's life.

Müller further mentioned that Linge and Rattenhuber knew about the double as did Goebbels, but Bormann and Guensche were not told. It appears also that General Mohnke was somehow involved in the conspiracy due to his later cover-up actions.

Following his entry into the bunker on the evening of April 22, 1945, the new "Hitler" was kept very isolated and was allowed to see only few and select persons. Bormann, since he was not told, was somewhat confused by the double. He remarked to Müller on April 23: "The chief looks very different, Müller, do you think he might have had some kind of a stroke?" General Weidling, who did not really know the real Hitler, remarked to a Russian wr correspondent, Lew Slavin, that he saw "Hitler" for the first time on April 24 1945, when he (Weidling) was appointed commander of the Berlin forces:

"As I now saw the Fuehrer I was astonished at his appearance, he was a human wreck, his head shook, his hands trembled, and his speech was hardly distinglishable."

He added,

"...there was an atmosphere of mistrust and there were likewise rumors abounding that proclaimed Hitler was no longer Hitler but his double!"

To quote from Joachim Fest's book: "Since Hitler's return to the Chancellery, there was evidence that something secret was going on."[6]

Dr. Schenck, who met the new Hitler on April 29 for the first time, stated:

"The pathetic man that I saw bore little resemblance to the old, mesmerizing idol of the masses that was so familiar to millions."

A similar observation was made by Captain Gerhard Boldt[29] an Adjutant of General Krebs during the last bunker days. He observed:

"His (the supposed Hitler's) posture was more bent then ever, his gait still more shuffling. The old flicker in his eyes had disappeared. Now his features were all flaccid, he looked exactly like a sick old man".

Traudl Junge's, (who was one of Hitler's last two secretaries) memoirs is also quite revealing. She states (after April 26th):

"His (Hitler's) right hand shakes as he lifts a spoon or fork to his mouth, he has difficulty getting out of his chair, and when he walks his feet drag over the floor."

Even more startling is her statement:

"We smoked a great deal, everywhere, whether the *Fuehrer* was with us or not. The thick cigarette smoke no longer bothered him."

The real Hitler never tolerated smoking in his presence.

At midnight on April 22, Albert Speer tried to talk to Hitler again before he returned to Wilnack, but he was told Hitler was asleep. This was quite unusual, since the real Hitler hardly went to bed before 3 A.M. Another curiosity was that contrary to the real Hitler, his double had breakfast at 8:.30 A.M. instead of around noon! While the real Hitler's military conferences started only after noon (due to his late sleeping habits) some early conferences began already around 10:30 a.m.[30]

Also quite unlike the real Hitler, who gave very precise military orders to his staff and his generals, his double was not trained in the art of warfare. Therefore he only issued platitudes such as "you must quickly execute all relief attacks", and "Advance on all fronts." Boldt reported hearing similar platitudes, such as, "The Third Army will make use of all available forces for this offensive …"[31].Even Minister Goebbels' coaching did not help here having had no military experience himself although Goebbels had many closed door conversations with this substitute Hitler, according to Gerda Christian, one of the remaining secretaries.

As told by McKale, again, General Weidling described the new Hitler as "a sick weakling hardly able to stand up or walk, manipulated by Goebbels."[7] Others stated that "Hitler" often closeted himself with Bormann and Goebbels."

As the German magazine *Spiegel* reported on January 10, 1966, in an understatement: "His (Hitler's) span of practical concern has narrowed." Thus he did not impress the remaining local military commanders during the brief military situation conferences *after* April 22. To quote General Mohnke from April 29:

"Hitler's midnight briefing had been short, desultory, and uninformative."

He further stated to O'Donnell:

"Throughout the whole talk I was sitting almost at his (the double's) side, perhaps three or four feet away. But he was either gazing at the wall or looking down at the floor. After the first ten minutes, our talk ceased to be a conversation.[8]"

This description certainly does not fit the Hitler who was at the same place three days earlier!

On April 30, the double issued an order (undoubtedly dictated by Goebbels) to General Weidling to authorize a break-out from Berlin for the remaining troops. Curiously, this order was typed on Hitler's personal letterhead, contrary to the normal practice! An earlier breakout request, on April 28, also by General Weidling, was brusquely rebuffed by Goebbels without even bothering to consult Hitler. This he would never have done had the real Hitler been present!

HITLER'S ESCAPE

Here is an apt description by Dr. Schenck who, on April 29, was asked by Prof. Haase to consult with the double, taking two nurses along. He testified:

"I was shaken a bit since I had never seen my Fuehrer before, except from an admiring distance. I knew, of course that this was Adolf Hitler and no *Doppelgänger*...(double)."

(This was rather disingenuous; he must have said this to please his interrogators, since he had no way of knowing the truth, having never met the real Hitler before). He then continued:

"Hatless, he was still wearing the familiar, once spotless, natty gray tunic with green shirt and long black trousers. He wore his golden party badge and his World War One Iron Cross on his left breast pocket. But the human being buried in these sloppy, food-stained clothes had completely withdrawn into himself. I could see his hunched spine, the curved shoulders that seemed to twitch and suddenly to tremble. He struck me as agonizing. Hitler seemed hardly able to shuffle the two paces forward to greet us. His eyes, although he was looking directly at me, said nothing. They did not seem to be focusing. The whites were bloodshot. His handshake was listless. At fifty-six the Fuehrer was a palsied, physical wreck, his face wrinkled like a mask, all yellow and gray."

General Müller hinted to his interrogators, "The double was drugged, likely by Prof. Haase."[9] This may explain the new Hitler's obviously listless impression he made on Schenck and others. Drugging was also suspected by Ambassador Hewel, who was reported to have said that Professor Haase may have given Hitler strong tranquilizing shots since the Fuehrer had very calm, even placid, periods during the last days.

The description of this Hitler's soiled uniform is rather revealing. This is in stark contrast to the real Hitler who was very particular when it came to his personal appearance. He also was very keen on personal hygiene. For example, he would always rinse his mouth after every meal.[10]

Schenck stayed in the bunker and later that night, after some drinking bouts, had to visit a toilet. The upper toilet happened to be clogged so he proceeded to walk to the lower level of the bunker towards the Fuehrer's quarters. To his astonishment, the two security guards normally guarding the entrance door were gone and he was able to walk by Hitler's sitting room unmolested, where he saw, what he believed to be, Hitler in an intense conversation with Prof. Haase.[11] It is interesting to note here how security had lapsed since the departure of the real Hitler!

Dr. Schenck observed that while sitting on a table, the new Hitler held his steel-rimmed glasses in his hand. This is another curiosity, since the real Hitler's glasses were nickel rimmed. As Minister Speer noticed, there was a distinct change in Hitler's daily routine. Now there were no more of the usual midnight conferences that Hitler was so fond of. At nighttime, once the busiest of hours, there were few souls about in the lower bunker.

During his walk-by observation, Dr. Schenck diagnosed that the substitute Hitler suffered from Parkinson's disease! General Mohnke who knew the real Hitler quite well, later ridiculed that statement.

Colonel von Below, Hitler's air force liaison officer, stated in his memoirs that Hitler often relapsed into apathy during the final days (after April 22nd). He further stated that Hitler virtually entered into seclusion and that he no longer interfered in the proceedings. Hitler's mood was unstable and one could not easily follow his thinking.

Let's compare the above physical condition and

appearance of the Hitler double to those of the real Fuehrer:

The real Hitler did have some slight tremors in his left arm and left leg, following the bomb explosion on July 20, 1944. He also suffered a sinus infection in September of 1944, followed by a bout of jaundice, which left him very weak and frail. However, he seemed to have recovered sufficiently so that he rarely saw a doctor during the first months of 1945. The only complaint was redness of the eyes and he had his valet Linge administer drops of cocaine solution.[12]

According to David Irving describing the real Hitler;

"On March 30, 1945, after issuing a clear-sighted appraisal of the situation... His malevolently brilliant mind was still functioning.[13]"

Similar statements were made by a Navy Commander Luedde-Neurath who attended the April 20 conference (when the real Hitler was still in Berlin) and who recorded in his diary: "Hitler's speech and eyes were as expressive as ever. His spiritual elasticity appeared preserved. He was not insane."[14] His doctors too were unanimous in agreeing that his sanity remained intact until the end, even though his blood-shot eyes (probably caused by the dusty bunker atmosphere) became so poor that he had to put on his spectacles even to read documents typed on special big-faced typewriters. As Joachim Fest writes:

"Frail as he was, he still preserved something of his magnetic powers...,"

and he gives as an example:

"When in March of 1945 Gauleiter Forster visited Hitler and was very much in despair about the Russian attack on his city of Danzig. Yet after only a brief conversation with Hitler, Forster's mood was completely transformed towards the positive!"[15]

Notes taken by C. Schröder, one of Hitler's secretaries, mentioned that her boss took anti-gas tablets and his doctors, Professors Brandt and Hasselbach told Hitler that this might have caused the occasional tremors in his left hand.

While it is possible for a double to fake a trembling hand, it is of course not possible to duplicate a brilliant mind. This was obvious from the vague and listless orders that Hitler's double issued. As a result, the generals, sensing a power vacuum disobeyed all orders after the Fuehrer's April 22 departure and followed their own strategy of survival.

As to the physical impairments, we have photographs of the real Hitler inspecting a group of Hitler Youth receiving medals for fighting the Russian troops. Here he is seen standing, walking and touching some of the boys in his heavy overcoat on his fifty-sixth birthday on April 20, 1945.[16] He was seen smiling, talking, and apparently relaxed and seemingly in good spirits. Probably the last photo shown of Hitler pictures him standing erect and with his hands behind his back together with his adjutant, Schaub, while inspecting bomb damage at the Chancellery on April 21, 1945.[17] He also had no problems climbing the forty-eight steps of the heavy iron spiral staircase out of the bunker. There exists also a photo of Hitler taken on April 1st inside the bunker, where Hitler greets Field Marshal Schörner. This photo again reveals no physical deterioration and it shows Hitler apparently quite well and smiling.

In papers, part of an FBI dossier on Hitler, is a translation dated December 6, 1945 of a diary of Hitler's physician (likely Dr. Morell) entitled "1944 Daily Treatment of Adolf".

In an entry of November 28, 1944, for example, it says: "F. (fuehrer) gone for vigorous walk of about 1 hour", and in the last entry, on December 31st, 1944 he wrote: "F. has become almost entirely calm. Trembling of l. arm or hand now only quite slight". Incidentally Hitler's Cholesterol was only 182 during that time period.

The testimony of Sergeant Mich, the last telephone switchboard operator in the bunker, which was broadcast on the US Discover TV channel in 2005 is very important. He stated that during the last (April 1945) days Hitler appeared changed in his appearance and he seemed to lack his normal vigor (pointing to the presence of a double). He also stated that Martin Bormann instructed Mich on April 27th, 1945, that he should route all phone calls from Dr J. Goebbels first to him, instead of directly to Hitler. Such an affront would have been intolerable, and would have been sternly rebuked by the "real" Hitler.

As to Hitler's stamina, I quote from J. Goebbels diary,[18] it states in an entry dated March 30, 1945:

I have the impression the Fuehrer is greatly overworked in the last few days. During the last 24 hours, for instance, he had only two hours of sleep.

And on April 3:

He is doing the utmost to pull his military staff together and to fill them with confidence for the future. He is tirelessly preaching the spirit of battle and resistance...

It seems obvious that the new "Hitler" (the double) did not

possess this energy, nor had he real power. An example of this was, that when Goering sensed the power vacuum in Berlin, he sent his famous telegram to the Fuehrer on April 23, giving what he thought was an ultimatum to Hitler to reply before 10 P.M.., otherwise he, Goering, would take over as Chancellor of Germany. Bormann, who disliked Goering, immediately took this opportunity and (falsely claiming: in Hitler's name) ordered Goering to be arrested by the SS troops. Bormann's handwritten telegram survived the war, according to D. Irving.[19] During these days (after April 22), Goebbels and Bormann were the real powerbrokers and made all the decisions. This is apparent from Bormann's signed message (not "Hitler's") to Admiral Doenitz during the morning of April 30 (prior to Hitler's supposed "suicide"), to inform him that Himmler tried to make peace, against orders, using Sweden as mediator.[20] There also seems to be some questions regarding the famous testament of Hitler dated April 29, 1945[21] which was witnessed by Bormann, Goebbels, Krebs and Burgdorf.[22] According to G. Junge (Hitler's youngest secretary) Hitler (the double) dictated his testament to me from "notes". James P. O'Donnell strongly suggests that these were notes written by Goebbels, matching exactly his style and phraseology. As a matter of fact, Goebbels even went so far as to add his own political testament as an appendix to the "Hitler" document. There seemed to be a touch of vanity in this undertaking. He probably needed to explain why Doenitz was chosen as Hitler's successor instead of him.

Yet, when we look at Hitler's signature on the political testament,[23] we see the same small, but clearly written signature, so familiar from other previous documents. This could not have been signed on April 29, at four a clock in the morning by a tottering, unsteady and trembling "Hitler" as Dr. Schenck described him on the same day, unless, of course, a facsimile signature was used![24] It is also unlikely that the substitute Fuehrer was up at four o'clock in the morning.

Here are the final bunker communications:

Martin Bormann, instead of Hitler, sent this telegram to Admiral Doenitz on April 30, 1945:

The Fuehrer appointed you, Herr Admiral, as his successor in place of Reichsmarshall Goering. Confirmation in writing follows. You are hereby authorized to take any measures which the situation demands. Bormann.

The end came on April 30, in the afternoon. Here is the most likely scenario of what happened: Dr. Stumpfegger gave the double his daily customary injection, except this time it was most likely poison and the double soon slumped over on the sofa of the living room, dead. To make sure he was dead, General Rattenhuber probably then shot the double in the forehead, using the double's own 7.65 caliber Walther pistol.[25]

Now Hitler's double of Hitler was dead. It appears from Russian investigations, that he was poisoned and then shot in the forehead, to make sure. This confirms Rattenhuber's statement to his Russian captors that Hitler was shot. It also verifies the story told to his Russians interrogators by the SS Guard Ackermann.

On May 1, 1945, at 2.45 P.M., the following additional message was sent to Doenitz:

Fuehrer died yesterday at 3:30 P.M. In his will dated April 29, he appoints you as President of the Reich, Goebbels as Reich Chancellor, Bormann as Party Minister, Seyss-Inquart as Foreign Minister. The will, by order of the Fuehrer, is being sent to you and to Field Marshal Schoerner and out of Berlin for safe custody. Bormann will try to reach you today to explain the situation. Form and timing of the announcement to the Armed Forces and the public is left to your discretion. Acknowledge. Goebbels – Bormann.

What is very curious about the latter message is, why would Hitler appoint Goebbels as Chancellor knowing quite well that Goebbels was going to commit suicide on the very same day!

Also, there was no hint of how Hitler died. Of course, the official suicide story only surfaced five months later, when the apparent escape of Hitler became an embarrassment for the Allies.

Here are summaries of the salient behavior and appearances of both Hitler and his double from the observations of the surviving witnesses both shortly before and after April 22, 1945.[26]

HITLER'S ESCAPE

HITLER BEFORE AND ON APRIL 22, 1945	"HITLER" AFTER APRIL 22, 1945.
Alert	Dull, drowsy
Could climb forty-eight steps to the bunker exit.	Hardly able to climb two steps
Could issue detailed military orders	Could utter only generalities
Slept late	Had breakfast at 8.30 A.M.
Preferred noon or late night conferences.	Had early morning conferences.
Issued verbal and written orders	Orders were issued only by Goebbels or Bormann in "Hitler's" name.
Had lunch with Eva Braun	Avoided all social contact with the (substitute) Eva Braun.
Dresses neatly	Wore uniform soiled with food stains[27]
Took customary half hour walks in the bunker garden	Never left the bunker.
Never tolerated cigarette smoking.	Allowed smoking.

It seems impossible that such a drastic personality change could occur within less than twenty-four hours. We have therefore to assume that the Hitler that was present in the bunker between April 22 and April 30, 1945 was indeed a double.

It is very puzzling why the presence of Hitler's double has received such scant attention by established historians despite the official Russian photographs of his existence.

Why, for example, were the witnesses never asked, "Who shot the double and who buried him?" Maybe the answer to all of this is that the whole story of Hitler's suicide would have collapsed if one were to admit that there was indeed a double in the bunker.

Notes

[1] Douglas, Gregory, *Gestapo Chief, The 1948 Interrogation of Heinrich Müller*, James Bender Publishing, 1995.

[2] Brown, Anthony Cave, *The Last Hero, Wild Bill Donovan*, Vintage Books, a division of Random House, 1984.

[3] Douglas, Gregory, *Gestapo Chief, The 1948 Interrogation of Heinrich Mueller*, James Bender Publishing, 1995.

[4] Brown, Anthony Cave, *The Last Hero, Wild Bill Donovan*, Vintage Books, a division of Random House, 1984.

[5] Joachimsthaler, Anton, *The Last Days Of Hitler*, Cassell & Co., London, 1995, p. 257.

[6] Fest, Joachim C., *Hitler*, A Harvest Book., Harcourt Inc., 1973.

[7] McKale, Donald M., *Hitler The Survival Myth*, Cooper Square Press, 1981.

[8] O'Donnell, James, P. *The Bunker*, Da Capo Press, 1978.

[9] Douglas, Gregory, *Gestapo Chief, The 1948 Interrogation of Heinrich Mueller*, James Bender Publishing, 1995.

[10] Schröder, Christa, *Er War Mein Chef*, second edition, Georg Müller Verlag, Germany, 1985.

[11] Prof. Haase was one of the substitute doctors responsible for Hitler's health. In April 1945 he was in charge of the field hospital located in the cellars of the Chancellery. Haase was taken prisoner by the Russian troops on May 3rd,and was taken to Russia, where he died in the fall of 1945.

[12] Irving, David, *Hitler's War*, Avon Books, a division of Hearst Corp., 1990.

[13] Ibit.

[14] McKale, Donald M., *Hitler The Survival Myth*, Cooper Square Press, 1981

[15] Fest, Joachim C., *Hitler*, A Harvest Book. Harcourt, Inc., 1973.

[16] Taylor, Blayne, *Guarding The Fuehrer*, Pictorial Histories Publishing Company, 1993, p. 242, American Heritage, *Pictorial History Of World War II*, Heritage Publishing Co. Inc., 1966, p. 574.

[17] *Chronik Der Deutschen*, Chronik Verlag, Germany, 1983, p. 926.

[18] Trevor-Roper, Hugh, *Final Entries, 1945. The Diaries of Joseph Goebbels*, G. P. Putnam's Sons, 1978.

[19] Irving, David, *Hitler's War*, Avon Books, a division of Hearst Corp., 1990.

[20] Doenitz, Karl, *Memoirs: Ten Years and Ten Days*, Da Capo Press, Inc., 1997, p. 440–441.

[21] *Chronik Der Deutschen*, Chronik Verlag, Germany, 1983, p. 926.

[22] None of these witnesses survived.

[23] *Ibit,*, p. 926.

[24] Some facsimiles are, especially lithographed, very deceptive. This is true of many Hitler's documents. From: K. W. Rendell, *History Comes To Life*, University of Oklahoma Press, 1995.

[25] Unlike the real Hitler, who used to carry a 6.35 mm caliber pistol, the double had a larger 7. 65 mm pistol in a holster.

[26] The comments refer to the real Hitler before April 22, the date of his disappearance and for the double thereafter.

[27] He even wore darned socks.

[29] Boldt, Gerhardt, *HITLER'S LAST DAYS*, Pen and Swords c Books, Ltd, Barnsley, UK,, 2005, p. 141.

[30] Ibit.,p. 141, 145.

[31] Ibit., p. 142.

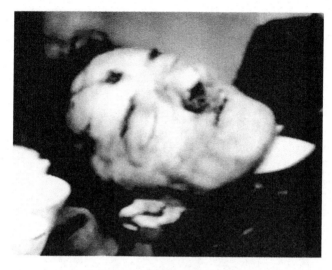

A photo of the dead Hitler's double.
Note, bullet hole in forehead.

On 2 May 1945, Russian Officers and camera men gloating
over the assumed corpse of Hitler. They discovered their
error two days later. It was the body of Hitler's double.

5 | THE "SUICIDE" ON APRIL 30

We now come to the more puzzling and contradictory aspects of this apparent murder and suicide story. Here we encounter many totally different versions of what was supposed to have happened on that day.

The official version widely accepted by the then Western powers and their media outlets was based on a report, later published as a book, by Sir Hugh Trevor-Roper.[1] He was later appointed a Regius Professor of modern History at Oxford and during the war was working for British Intelligence (MI5). This man was chosen by the British Government to conduct an investigation in response to Russian statements that Hitler was alive in Spain, or even in Westphalia (a German State in the British occupied zone). Western newspapers, at that time, carried those stories widely.

This was bad public relations for the United States and Great Britain at the end of a terrible war, and it had to be counteracted as soon as possible. Trevor-Roper, in his Royal Territorial Army officer's uniform, was given all access to prisoners of war and other potential witnesses (except to the most important ones, now in Russian prisons). He was only briefly allowed to see the bunker (which he found utterly neglected with two or three inches of water covering the floor, concluding that there had been no forensic investigation done by the Russians). He also had the full co-operation of the U.S. military.

In his press release on November 1, 1945, and after little more than four weeks of investigation, "this droll man, and a master of tart understatement", as O'Donnell called him, managed to convince the international press that Hitler was indeed dead, despite the absence of any corpse.

Here is the gist of his report:

Available evidence sifted by British Intelligence and based largely on eyewitness accounts shows – as conclusive as possible without bodies – that Hitler and Eva Braun died shortly after 2:30 A.M. (most say it was 3.30 P.M.) on April 30, 1945, in the bunker of the Reich Chancellery, their bodies being buried just outside the bunker.

On the evening of April 29 Hitler married Eva Braun, the ceremony being performed by an official from the Propaganda Ministry in a small conference room in the bunker....

At about 2:30 A.M. on April 30 Hitler said goodbye to about twenty people, about ten of them women, whom he summoned from the old bunker in the Old and New Reich Chancelleries. He shook hands with the women and spoke to most of them.

On the same day, at about 2.30 P.M., though the time is uncertain, orders were sent to the transport office requiring the immediate dispatch to the bunker of 200 liters of petrol. Between 160 and 180 liters of petrol were collected and deposited in the garden just outside the emergency exit of the bunker. At about the same time Hitler and Eva Braun made their last appearance alive. They went around the bunker and shook hands with their immediate entourage and retired to their own apartments, where they both committed suicide, Hitler shooting himself, apparently through the mouth, Eva Braun apparently, by taking poison, though she was supplied with a revolver.

After the suicide the bodies were taken into the garden, just outside the bunker, by Goebbels, Bormann, perhaps Colonel Stumpfegger, and one or two others. Hitler was wrapped in a blanket, presumably because he was bloody.

The bodies were placed side by side in the garden about three yards from the emergency exit of the bunker and drenched with petrol. Because of the shelling, the party withdrew under the shelter of the emergency exit and a petrol-soaked and lighted rag was thrown on the bodies, which at once caught fire. The burial party then stood at attention, gave the Hitler salute, and retired.

From there on, the evidence is more circumstantial. How often the bodies were re-soaked or how long they burned, is not known. One witness was informed that they burned until nothing was left; more probably they were charred until they were unrecognizable, and the bones broken up and probably buried.

The above evidence is not complete, but it is positive, circumstantial, consistent, and independent. There is no evidence whatever to support any theories that have been circulated and which presuppose that Hitler is still alive. All such stories which have been reported have been investigated and have been found quite baseless; and some of them have been admitted by their authors to have been pure fabrication.

All in all this was not a bad report aside from some minor errors (such as that E. Braun had a pistol instead of a revolver, and the timing of the marriage was wrong, etc.), and considering that he could not interview the key witnesses being either dead or Russian prisoners.

However, what is remarkable about this story is the part of Hitler and Eva Braun sitting in "their own apartments" and Hitler shooting himself, while Eva Braun apparently poisoned herself. Where did this come from? The only witnesses Trevor-Roper had to interview about what went on *inside* the Bunker where Erich Kempka, Gerda Christian and Else Krueger (Bormann's secretary). Kempka admitted sheepishly to O'Donnell in 1974 that he was not even among those present in the corridor at that critical moment! Neither were Else Krueger and G. Christian. It is more than likely that all three persons were at that time in their living quarters, which were located on the upstairs bunker floor. Therefore, they could only tell what they might have snapped up from conversations with the valet Linge, and others. For example, G. Christian, one of Hitler's secretaries, stated that she learned of the Hitler suicide from Linge and T. Junge, another secretary, learned it from SS Major Guensche. Junge further claimed that, according to Guensche, Hitler's ashes were collected in a box that was given to Youth Leader Arthur Axmann. This was of course denied by Axmann.

No bodies of Hitler, or of Eva Braun, were ever found.[2] Please note also that the whole Trevor-Roper report stated quite clearly, at the onset, that the investigation was made "without bodies", that is without any physical evidence whatsoever! However, it fits with the Nordon Report stating that Trevor-Roper, at one time, was told by the Russians that they had found two burned bodies (See chapter titled: "What the Russians Discovered"), except that this conflicts with one of Trevor-Roper's witnesses' statement "that the bodies were burned till nothing was left".

Yet this story of the dual suicide in Hitler's anteroom nevertheless became thereafter something of a historical fact. Even the Russians adopted this version, although with some minor variation. This was done only later in 1968, long after Stalin's death. Stalin, the Russian leader at that time (1945), quite likely knew of Hitler's escape. However, Trevor-Roper, being annoyed that the Russians would not accept his own findings, later dismissed Stalin's insistence that Hitler was alive, by stating: "Stalin had decided to suppress the documents and falsify the evidence in 1945." Maybe out of wounded pride he further argued: "Either (Stalin) was genuinely unconvinced by the Russian inquiry, or he deliberately falsified its results for political purposes." Trevor Roper, as did many others, also suspected the accuracy of the much later (1968) Russian autopsy report on the two "burned" corpses. Yet, despite his misgivings, he chose to include the Russian version of what happened to Hitler in his third book. A grateful Great Britain made Trevor-Roper a peer of the realm.

Trevor-Roper's account of the carrying of the bodies up to the garden, and the subsequent cremation, was apparently based on the testimony of a Hermann Karnau, who was supposed to have been an SS member (he really was a police detective).

There is another major flaw to the story. Kempka, Hitler's chief chauffeur, told O'Connell in 1973 that when he was requested to supply petrol on April 30, he said there was insufficient petrol left.[3] He only could obtain about 180 liters. Still, he had sufficient petrol the following day (May 1st) to burn the bodies of Joseph and Magda Goebbels almost to cinders. However, if one considers that Mülller's plan was to bury the unburned body of Hitler's double, in order for it to be found by the Russian troops, then Kempka's statements that there was only sufficient gasoline to burn two bodies (that of Dr. and Mrs. Goebbels) make sense. However, all these stories have to be taken with a grain of salt. For example, Kempka explained apparent contradictions in his story by saying, "Back in forty-five to save my own skin, I told American and British interrogators just about anything or everything they wanted to hear."

Here is another version of the events, according to Toland[4]:

Guensche called Kempka that he needed two hundred liters of gasoline. Impossible, replied Kempka all the gas is buried in the Tiergarten and we cannot get it due to artillery fire. At 3.30 P.M., on April 30, 1945, Hitler picked up a Walther pistol. He was alone in the anteroom[4] of his quarters with Eva Braun. She was already dead. She was on a couch slumped over the armrest, poisoned. A second Walther lay on the red carpet, unfired. Hitler sat at a table. He put the pistol barrel in his mouth and fired. In the conference room, Bormann, Guensche and Linge heard the shot. They hesitated momentarily, then broke into Hitler's anteroom.

This version was apparently based on Kempka's original testimony in 1945, later retracted by Kempka. This was also disputed by Arthur Axmann, who stated; "I was standing right there, as close to the door as possible, but I certainly heard no shot." Kempka also told his first American and British interrogators in 1945 that, when looking into the suicide room, he saw both corpses and he said, "....it was clear to me that the Fuehrer and Miss Braun shot themselves." And later: "While carrying Miss Braun upstairs I saw blood trickling out of her breast." This apparent contradiction in Kempka's testimonies was also noticed by the *London Times,* stating that Kempka's statement: "...left the mystery of Hitler's end as undecided as before."

The alert reader will have by now discovered that each of the surviving key players in this drama Linge, Kempka, Rattenhuber and Guensche told a different story about what was supposed to have happened regarding the suicide! The question is, why? Perhaps it was too hectic, or there was insufficient time to rehearse their story sufficiently for a foolproof cover-up. Sergeant Mich, the switchboard operator in the bunker claimed in a 2005 broadcast TV show, that he saw Hitler slumped in an arm chair and Eva Braun on the sofa; this is different from the "official" story that both had died on the sofa.

Another version, pieced together by O'Donnell and based primarily on information given by Prof. Haase to Dr. Schenck, went as follows:

Hitler sat down on the left-hand corner of the narrow sofa. Next he took out of his tunic pocket two poison vials. One he placed on the table between the pistol and a vase. The other he put into his mouth. His bride, Eva, was seated in the other corner of the blue and white sofa. Eva put a poison capsule in her mouth. She apparently then bit into the capsule. Hitler must have put the muzzle of his black Walther directly to his graying left temple, right angle at eyebrow level. He then squeezed the trigger and simultaneously bit into his capsule.

Heinz Linge was supposed to wait ten minutes before opening the door to Hitler's anteroom; instead he dashed up the stairs and was the first to enter.

Note, if anything Linge would have dashed *downstairs*, since Hitler's rooms were on the lower level of the two-story bunker.

There are several questionable aspects to this story. First, it is based on hearsay; Prof. Haase was not supposed to be present when this apparent suicide happened. Secondly, it would have been nearly impossible to simultaneously bite the poison capsule and to shoot one self. Thirdly, if no shot was heard (see previous testimony, and the fact that the room was closed by a heavy metal door), how did Linge know that the suicide had happened before he entered the room? Finally, here we have Hitler shot in the temple instead of through the mouth! Another absurdity about part of Linge's and Schenck's testimony was "that Hitler shot himself with his left hand in his left temple".

First of all, Hitler was right-handed, and secondly, his left hand sometimes trembled.

What is the strangest part of all these stories is the fact that the above witnesses could describe exactly what was happening inside a room whose soundproof door was closed and where the only occupants were dead! We must therefore conclude that at least part of this testimony is pure speculation.

Rattenhuber later told his Russian captors that Hitler had been given the "coup de grâce" with his own pistol, in case the poison did not work. This testimony conflicted with

Linge and Guensche's testimony to the Russians and, as a result, he got the latter two into a lot of trouble. Yet Rattenhuber's story may have well applied to the killing of Hitler's double.

James O'Donnell admitted, that it is possible, that Linge and Guensche might have been lying.[5] That is of course a distinct possibility since according to the SS General Müller, at least Linge was a co-conspirator in the apparent murder of Hitler's double as we will see later. As such he must have been very careful in all of his testimonies in order to avoid being prosecuted later in court for being an accessory to the murder of Hitler's double.

The East German writer, Rosanow, in 1956 published a book that apparently was heavily censored by Moscow, stating that "Hitler shot himself in the mouth, Eva Braun had taken poison." He also showed the familiar photo of the corpse (discovered on May 2 and well preserved) of Hitler 's double, proclaiming it was the real thing, this despite the official Russian version (after 1968) that Hitler's body was partly burned! It also ignored the bullet hole in the forehead of the double.

In his book *Hitler, The Survival Myth*[6], Donald McKale gives yet another version, quoting Robert Waite, an American historian:

Linge had discovered Hitler in the death room with his hands folded carefully in his lap. The Fuehrer took poison and then someone, but not Linge or Guensche, as the Russians assumed, had shot him. He surmised that it was Eva Braun who shot Hitler. This happened at 3.30 on the afternoon of April 30.

Now we come to the latest version of what happened. This is the result of Anton Joachimsthaler's well researched book[7] which was published only in 1995:

> After evaluating all the testimony and photographs, and after considering all the known circumstances *in situ*, Hitler (on the right) and Eva Braun (on the left) were sitting on the narrow, 1.70 m long sofa in Hitler's living room-cum-office before the suicide.
>
> Eva Braun-Hitler then bit down on the prussic acid ampoule and probably fell over on to Hitler sideways. Subsequently Hitler lifted his pistol to his temple and pulled the trigger. After the shot his body then remained seated between Eva Braun and the armrest of the sofa with the head canted slightly forward to the right. The dropping right arm let go of the pistol, which fell to the floor. With the shot into the temple, blood dripped onto the armrest of the sofa and then flowed in a copious amount onto the rug in front of the armrest of the sofa.

Joachimsthaler left no doubt that he believes that the bodies were those of Adolf Hitler and Eva Braun. His conviction is based on what he claims is an unmistakable identification, by the witnesses; in particular those of Guensche, Kempka, Hofbeck and others, because Hitler's head was partially uncovered and his lower limbs with the black trousers, black socks and shoes were exposed. Eva Braun- Hitler's corpse, in contrast, was uncovered.

What shall we make of this? On the surface it all sounds very plausible. There is however one puzzling aspect of the last version. How come blood from Hitler trickled down on to the left armrest of the sofa (as photos confirm), on the side where Eva Braun was sitting?

However, if we assume that the person who was shot was in reality Hitler's double, then the testimony by Linge, Guensche and Axmann make sense (including the continuing contradictions in detail). Remember these witnesses were sworn (according to Russian accounts) to pretend that the real Hitler committed suicide. The additional fact is that the Russians found this double, who was most likely shot inside the bunker.

We don't know who the so-called Eva Braun was, but remember there was another testimony that her body too was covered. As to the *credible* testimony of the other witnesses, who carried Hitler upstairs to the garden, we know that only Hitler's forehead and not his face, was uncovered. Consider also the great similarity in appearance between Hitler and his double. Finally we have the pants, the socks and the shoes. Any forensic expert would laugh at this kind of "positive identification". After all, the first thing you do with a double is to dress him in a like manner! Note also that according to testimony given in a German court, none of forty witnesses could positively identify Hitler's alleged corpse. Another point to remember is that if Linge or Guensche tells everybody in the bunker that Hitler has just committed suicide, then why should not the other personnel in the bunker believe this and automatically assume that the corpse being carried out was the real Hitler? While there were traces of blood on the armrest of the sofa in Hitler's living room, there was also a large single pool of blood (ten to twelve inches in diameter) on the red carpet at least two feet in front of the sofa. This could not possibly have come from the blood trickling down the armrest.

Here is my final argument: Even though the blood-stained carped from Hitler's office was burned in the garden on orders from Linge, there was (according to photographs) sufficient blood on the arm rest of the sofa to allow for a blood sample. The results of such tests were never published, if the Russians ever indeed took blood samples. The likely reason: the blood was not Adolf Hitler's type.[8]

The official history of the U.S. Army states flatly: "Hitler shot himself with a pistol."

So, if you are confused, you are not alone. We may certainly assume that there was one dead Fuehrer that afternoon. But it must have been Hitler's double. His was the *only* corpse found. According to Müller's testimony, the double was first drugged and then shot in the forehead using a Walther 7.65 mm pistol.

Was the story of the "official" suicide in Hitler's anteroom true? Most likely *not,* since, as we can see, it was based primarily on later recanted testimony and on a lot of hearsay. It is also uncorroborated by any forensic evidence, and, most importantly by the absence of any corpses!

In any case, it would have been difficult to conduct a thorough forensic investigation of the rooms in question, since the bunker was looted by Russian troops prior to the 2 P.M. arrival of the Russian intelligence troops. (It was reported that Russian women soldiers brandished the black-laced bras belonging to Eva Braun). Besides, there are reports that the Bunker hallways were partly flooded due to the shut-off of the utilities. Also, no bullets were ever found. We also have to consider the report from General Mohnke that he ordered Hitler's study to be burned by Captain Schwägermann on May 1. The room was set alight with gasoline, according to the testimony of the technician Hentschel, who was the last to leave the bunker. Hentschel further stated the steel door to the study was red hot and the rubber seals melted. Such a hot fire could have destroyed at least some of the evidence, at least in the anteroom.

A recent article by Ada Petrova and Peter Watson in the *Washington Post*, which was supposed to be the "full story" about Hitler's death, with new "evidence from secret Russian Archives", does not shed any more light on the story, but lists a number of fake sightings of Hitler among other known details. They stated that Trevor-Roper gave a lot of credence in his story to the existence of the Hitler testament and his wedding contract with Eva Braun (this wedding ceremony did not have one single surviving witness!). The authors stated: "The fact of the marriage tends to confirm the psychological portrait Trevor-Roper was putting together."(If you don't have enough facts, you substitute with psychology). While the authors of this article admit that "the Trevor-Roper account was necessarily incomplete and that there were many gaps to be filled in", they concluded that the book published by Trevor-Roper in 1947 "by rights ought to have solved the mystery once and for all, to have killed speculation for ever. It was meticulously researched, well written and by and large convincing. *But among several points left unresolved, one all-important matter has been remaining a mystery.*" [Emphasis added by this author]. Unfortunately the authors did not elaborate which matter remained a mystery.[9]

Returning to the surviving witnesses, please remember, that everybody was under tremendous pressure in those days. There was constant bombardment above, stifling air inside the bunker, and everybody was very scared of the Russian troops and concerned for their personal future. It must have been terrifying. As a result, there was heavy alcohol consumption.

On top of this, there later was the very tough interrogation by Russian and Western intelligence officers. Each one was trying to make the witness confirm his own pet theories and political agendas. For example, Guensche underwent hundreds of hours of interrogation and torture in a Moscow prison and he was promised instant release if he would change his story towards the ideas of their captors of what supposed to have happened in Berlin. Finally, there was the fear of giving incriminating evidence and possible later prosecution of some for apparently murdering Hitler's double.

Just in case I might have confused you with the previous narrative, here is a summary of the Hitler's alleged demise:

Source:	How Hitler Died: :
H. Trevor-Roper	Shot himself in the mouth
J. O'Donnell	Poisoned and shot himself in the left temple
E. Kempka	Shot himself
J. Toland	Shot himself in the mouth
Rattenhuber	Poisoned himself, then was shot by one of his guards*
Rosanow	Shot himself in the mouth
D. McKale	Took poison then was shot by one of his guards*
A. Joachimsthaler	Shot himself in the right temple.
Lev Bezymenski	Poisoned then shot by his guard*
Russian (SMERSH) Autopsy report:	Hitler poisoned himself.[10]

The methods of death marked with an asterisk seems most closely to agree with the appearance of the corpse of Hitler's double.

Here is a statement by Joachim Fest that sums it up pretty well: "What really happened (in the bunker) has by now become impossible to reconstruct."[11]

Dear reader, you now can choose the way Hitler supposedly met his death; either by shooting himself in the left temple, the right temple or in the mouth. Or, if you prefer, that he poisoned himself or better yet, that he poisoned and then shot himself. It would have been easy to solve this riddle, if the Russians had really found and investigated Hitler's corpse, even if partly cremated. Alas, that did not happen. It is interesting that each of the major historians interviewing surviving witnesses, namely Joachimsthaler, McKale, Toland and O'Donnel choose only the statement of only one selected key witness as to the means of Hitler's death. They did this despite the fact that all the witnesses contradicted each other. It seems that each historian believed his particular witness was the most trustworthy! This, of course implies that all others lied. Logically one might then say that all witnesses were lying.

It appears from the above tabulation that Müller's description of the way Hitler's double died, that he was first poisoned and then shot in the forehead, is correct. All the Russian statements also tend to confirm Müller's assertions.

It also would indicate that all other statements, as conflicting which each other as they are in telling how the real Hitler died, can be relegated to the realm of fantasy.

Finally, a lot of credence should be given to W. F. Heimlich, who (in 1945) was the Chief Intelligence Officer for the U.S. Army in Berlin.[13] He was assigned to cooperate with Trevor-Roper, from Britain's MI 5, to investigate Hitler's death. However, after investigating the matter, Heimlich came to a quite different conclusion from Trevor-Roper, who ignored him thereafter. He wrote on July 5th, 1947:

"I can state positively that I did not find Hitler nor did I find his physical remains, despite a thorough search of the area."

Heimlich further stated:

"...I cannot overstress the fact that I have never been able to find any reliable witness of Hitler's activities after April 22, 1945 – nine days before the date of his supposed suicide. Under these circumstances I could never understand, on what substance Trevor-Roper based his 'Official British Intelligence Report' on November 1, 1945[1] and the more so, because the bomb crater in the Garden of the Reichschancellory (sic)—where the Fuehrer was supposed to have been buried after being "cremated"—was not excavated for investigation until December 12, 1945, more than seven months after the surrender of Berlin".

Note, the date of April 22nd given above coincides with the date of Hitler's assumed escape. Furthermore, Heimlich stated:

"It is the opinion of qualified experts that it is impossible to destroy completely a human body burned in the open air."

He also discredited the story of two witnesses (Herman Karnau and Erich Mansfield), on whose testimonies Trevor-Roper relied in part, and I quote:

"Both were unreliable and, moreover, were not familiar with the Reich Chancellery area's bunker layout. When questioned thoroughly, they betrayed their lack of knowledge, even of the direction in which the entrance to the Fuehrerbunker faced".

Russian Troops investigating Hitler's study finding here distinct blood spots (circled), indicating Hitler's double was shot in the forehead with bullet piercing his cranium in back (see upper blood spots). Blood then trickled down on arm rest (second spot). The corpse then was laid down where the bleeding head produced the large mark on the floor.

On 16 September 2009, the HISTORY CHANNEL broadcasted a show entitled *Hitler's Escape*, based in part on the book *Hitler's Fate* by H. D. Baumann. As part of the investigations relating to the subject, the TV channel dispatched an expert to a Museum in Moscow housing memorabilia from the Fuehrer bunker. Among those was a scull supposedly belonging to Hitler (see illustration elsewhere). The expert was able to remove a portion of the skull, sufficient to extract DNA. A subsequent analyses in a US laboratory established that the scull, in reality, belonged to a young woman. There goes another legend!

Notes

[1] Trevor-Roper, Hugh, *Last Days of Hitler*, third edition, *The Times*, London, 1946.

[2] Brown, Anthony Cave, *The Last Hero*, *Wild Bill Donovan*, Vintage Books, a division of Random House, 1984.

[3] Toland, John, *The Last Days*, A Bantam Book/ Randam House, Inc., 1967

[4] According to other witnesses, the suicide happened in Hitler's study or living room, next to his anteroom.

[5] O'Donnell, James, *The Bunker*, DA CAPO Press, 1978

[6] McKale, Donald M., *Hitler The Survival Myth*, Cooper Square Press, 1981

[7] Joachimsthaler, Anton, *The Last Days Of Hitler*, Cassell & Co., London, 1995

[8] Irving, David, *Hitler's War*, Avon Books, a division of Hearst Corp., 1990

[9] Petrova, Ada and Watson, Peter, *The Death Of Hitler*, *Washington Post*, 7–6–2003

[10] Petrova, Ada, and Watson, Peter, *The Death Of Hitler*, *Washington Post*, 7-6-2003.

[11] Fest, Joachim, *Inside Hitler's Bunker*, Picador, Farrar, Strauss and Giroux, New York, 2002, pp. 116.

[12] *The HITLER BOOK , The secret Dossier Prepared for Stalin*, Public Affairs, New York, 2005, pp. 283.

[13] Moore, Herbert, and Barrett,, James, *Who Killed Hitler?* , The Booktab Press, NY, 1947, (Foreword).

6 | HITLER'S LAST WILL

Part of the clue to the puzzle of Hitler's escape may be found in his political testament.

Here is the official story. During the night of April 28, and following the midnight wedding reception, Hitler supposedly wrote both a political and one personal testament, typed in three sets, which he then supposedly signed at 4 o'clock on the morning of April 29, 1945.

As we mentioned previously, Traudl Junge, one of Hitler's two remaining secretaries, stated that the will was dictated to her from notes. She then wrote in shorthand, and later transcribed the text onto her typewriter. This was the first time this had ever happened to her, since the real Hitler always dictated to her while she was typing and without using any notes! All this, the notes and the style of dictation again points to the presence of a double. According to Ian Kershaw, while the will was being dictated, "Goebbels together with Bormann, kept bringing Fräulein Junge the names of additional ministers to type on to the list (the proposed members of a new government requested in the testament)."[1] The real Hitler would never have tolerated such interference!

The personal part of the will was rather short and discussed his marriage and his appreciation that "this girl entered this city, already besieged, of her own free will, in order to share my fate with me. At her request she is joining me in death as my wife..." Hitler also appointed Martin Bormann as executor of his will and requested him to assist his relatives and former secretaries.[2]

It ended by saying: I myself and my wife, chose death to

73

escape the disgrace of removal or surrender. It is our desire to be burned at once at the place in which I have performed the greater part of my daily work in the course of twelve years of service to my people.

While this personal testament suggests suicide, it actually does not say so. It also presupposes that Martin Bormann would have been able to escape from Berlin, how else could he perform his function as executor of his will? Finally, Hitler ordered that his body should be burned. This last statement fitted well with the agreed upon cover story of the dual suicide with subsequent cremation.

The political will is much longer and a part of the text accused the international Jewry and its accomplices for ruining the cities and monuments. It begins:

It is not true that I or anybody in Germany wanted war back in 1939. It was desired and provoked solely by those international politicians who either come from Jewish stock or are agents of Jewish interests. After all my offers of disarmament, posterity simply cannot pin any blame for this war on me...

After a struggle of six long years, which in spite of many setbacks will one day be recorded in our history books as the most glorious and valiant manifestation of the nation's will to live.

I cannot abandon this city, which is the German capital. Since we no longer have sufficient military forces to withstand enemy attacks on this city, and since our own resistance will be gradually exhausted fighting an army of blind automata, it is my desire to share the same fate that millions of other Germans have accepted and to remain here in this city...

He also reviewed the last twenty-five years of his struggle and its justification. However, what is more important to our story is that he named Admiral Doenitz as his successor for the post of President and he appointed Joseph Goebbels as Chancellor of the Reich. This portion of the will was faithfully passed on to Doenitz during the following day by Bormann in the form of a telegram. Otherwise, this testament expressed exactly Hitler's political outlook that he had years ago. Assuming that he was the author of this document, then he was simply trying to justify himself and his actions to the coming generations of Germans.

In this testament he hinted at dying in Berlin but left the method of his death open. However, reading this portion of his will and finding the dead double could then convince the Russians that he, Hitler, was indeed dead.

The trouble with this will is, that it could not have been written by Hitler's double, the only "Fuehrer" left in the bunker. First of all, there was little more than three hour's time between the break-up of the fake wedding party (the ceremony itself did not end till after midnight, followed by a reception). It would certainly take more than an hour just to dictate this lengthy, and for Hitler quite important, document, then it had to be transcribed from shorthand and finally edited; then, two additional copies had to be typed too. Finally, the double was not that familiar with the phraseology and the historical references made in the political will.

It was suggested by O'Donnell that the document was dictated using notes written by Dr. Joseph Goebbels.[3] That could not be true either. Why would Goebbels write a will to appoint himself Chancellor and then two days later commit suicide?

This brings us to the most puzzling part and that is: Why did the real Hitler write a will on April 29, to name Goebbels Chancellor knowing quite well (as everybody else in the bunker knew) that Goebbels planned to commit suicide together with his family, which he did two days later?

According to O'Donnell, Goebbels confided in mid February 1945 to his aid, Lieutenant von Oven: "Neither my wife nor a single one of my offspring will be among the survivors of the coming debacle."[4] This clearly shows that the suicide was planned for a long time.

There are only two logical explanations for these contradictions. First, that the will was a forgery. One fact that speaks for this assumption is, that the last two paragraphs alone, containing sixty words, include no less than six major spelling and grammatical errors. These errors are of such a nature that it appears a person made them, who was not too familiar with the German language a foreigner, for example. It is hard to believe that Hitler's remaining secretaries, who both had many years of experience, could have made such blatant spelling errors. It is even more unlikely that Hitler would have signed such a document, which had all the hallmarks of being typed by an eighth grader. As any dealer in autographs knows there are many forgeries on the market which are so well done that they easily pass as originals. Furthermore, intelligence services have plenty of specialists and equipment to produce false passports and other documents. Of interest in this connection is the report that Ernst Kaltenbrunner, the former head of the German State Security Service, was captured in May 1945, in the Austrian Alps. He was supposed to have with him one copy each of Hitler's personal and his political testament. The strange part about this story is, that Colonel von Bühlow, who gave it to Field Marshall Keitel, then in Northern Germany, carried the only set that got out of Berlin! General Mohnke taped it to his body then carried the other two sets of testaments out of the bunker. The Russians later captured Mohnke, on May 2, 1945. It therefore can be assumed that these only remaining two copies of the wills are kept in Russia. However, the assumption of a forgery was supposedly disproved by a U.S. forensic investigation of at least one of the original three copies, that were sent out of the bunker.

The second explanation is that the two documents were actually written some time *before* April 22, 1945, when Hitler thought he still could talk Goebbels out of the suicide idea (he certainly tried). Note also that Dr. Goebbels and his wife were listed as passengers on the original flight manifest to Barcelona, Spain. This, of course, also agrees with the story SS General Müller told his interrogators namely, that the will and the marriage contract were written and signed prior to Hitler's departure.[5] All Goebbels or Bormann had to do was to have the witnesses sign the documents. The double probably was not even asked to attend the 4 A.M. signing; at that time he was probably sound asleep.

Of course, there is still no explanation of the many typing errors in the document.

An FBI document number 65-53615-61 depicts a letter dated March 13, 1946 and signed by J. Edgar Hoover. It is addressed to the assistant Chief of Staff at the US War Department. Attached to this letter is a report of the FBI Laboratory "to verify the authenticity of the documents and the signature of Hitler" of three documents sent to the FBI on March 7th, 1946. These documents include Hitler's Certificate of Marriage, his Private Will and his Political Will. On the outset, it is amazing that such important documents could be analyzed in less than 6 days!

In the report, it was found that that the documents were partly glued to cardboard using rubber cement. Therefore, only some of the pages were removed for testing. It was further stated; "at no time was anything placed on the papers (in the nature of test reagent, solvents, adhesive or any other Laboratory material) such as might be applied in an examination". This certainly would preclude the examination of the type of ink used, the age of the signature, and whether or not a facsimile was used.

HITLER'S ESCAPE

The signatures were judged authentic solely by comparison to other specimens. Even this only applied to the signatures of Hitler, Bormann and Burgdorf. No comparison could be made as to the signatures of Goebbels, Eva Braun, Hans Krebs, and Claus von Bühlow, since no writing samples were available.

The Marriage Certificate was judged "the most questionable"; it was partly typed (instead of being a printed form, as was customary) and completed by hand.

The investigating report states: "The fact that the other documents are typed raises questions". Nevertheless it was concluded, "...the unusual way of preparing the document is evidence of genuiness rather than otherwise".

Other than a forgery, they can only be explained by the extreme pressure, the late hours, perhaps alcohol consumption and the knowledge that the real Hitler was no longer there. Then again, the published document showing these errors might have been a poor copy of the original wills. Yet we might well conclude that these puzzling aspects of the wills could be considered as additional evidence that the real Hitler was not in the bunker at the given time frame.

Here I would like to add some comments on, what I believe was a "fake" wedding. The ceremony was to have started shortly before midnight on April 28 and was said to have taken place in the small anteroom next to Hitler's living quarters. This anteroom was sealed by a soundproof steel door. A local notary, Walter Wagner, officiated. Besides him there were only Hitler, Eva Braun, Goebbels and Bormann in the room. All of these people were dead within the next three days; poor Wagner was shot dead within the next hour!

However, we can find in Fest's book,[6] a description of the whole speech by Wagner, and I quote:

I come here to the solemn act of matrimony. In the presence of the above-mentioned witnesses... I ask you, My Leader, Adolf Hitler, whether you are willing to enter into matrimony with Miss Eva Braun. If such is the case, I ask you to reply "yes".

Herewith I ask you, Eva Braun, whether you are willing to enter into matrimony with my Leader, Adolf Hitler. If such is the case, I ask you to reply "yes".

Now, since both these engaged persons have stated their willingness to enter into matrimony, I hereby declare the marriage valid before the law.

This verbatim quote of what went on behind closed doors is, to put it mildly, very puzzling, since there is not a single surviving witness to this scene. Again, we can assume that the only thing that went on here was that the wedding document, pre-signed by Hitler and Braun was then countersigned and dated by Wagner and the witnesses.

Of course this explains, why SS General Müller had Wagner liquidated within half an hour after the "ceremony".[7] If the Russians had caught him, he might have talked and exposed the whole "double spiel" by admitting that there was no "real" Hitler, and for that matter no "real" Eva Braun in the bunker. Otherwise, the wedding nicely reinforced the desired impression that Hitler and Braun were still in the bunker.

Following the "wedding", there was a reception in a small conference room. According to Fest, it was attended by the "newly weds", the secretaries, the adjutants and Miss Manzialy, Hitler's dietary cook for many years. This small party, attended only by low-level bunker insiders, enjoyed drinks and reminisced. It would have been interesting to know, whether the "Double" drank champagne. If he did, then his behavior would have been quite a departure from the habit of the teetotaler Hitler. Also, another strange fact is, why were Bormann and Goebbels absent on such a special occasion? We will never know. However, one explanation could be that it was beyond their dignity to socially associate themselves withh such a small fish as "Hitler" the Double. Besides, Goebbels was busy that night, writing, dictating and adding his personal testament to that of Hitler's.

As for Miss Manzialy, Hitler's cook, she also disappeared shortly thereafter. Rumor has it that she poisoned herself on May 2, 1945.[8]

Notes

[1] Kershaw, Ian, *Hitler*, W. W. Norton & Co., 2000.

[2] Fest, Joachim C., *Hitler*, A Harvest Book. Harcourt,, Inc., 1973.

[3] O'Donnell, James, P., *The Bunker*, Da Capo Press, 1978.

[4] Ibid.

[5] Douglas, Gregory, *Gestapo Chief, The 1948 Interrogation of Heinrich Müller*, James Bender Publishing, 1995.

[6] Fest, Joachim C., *Hitler*, A Harvest Book. Harcourt, Inc., 1973.

[7] Douglas, Gregory, *Gestapo Chief, The 1948 Interrogation of Heinrich Müller*, James Bender Publishing, 1995.

[8] Overy, Richard, *Interrogations, The Nazis In Allied Hands, 1945*, Penguin Putnam, Inc., 2001.

7 | SPEER THE ENIGMA

Despite the fact that Speer was Hitler's closest confidant and trusted advisor, Speer was treated very leniently at the
    Nuremberg War Crimes trials. This was in part due to his skillful exploitation of the animosity between the British and the Soviet prosecutor. [1]

His *mea culpa* was cleverly directed to admit his role in the prolongation of the war, yet denying any knowledge or participation of the Holocaust. The other story, which he skillfully inserted into the Nuremberg proceedings, is his alleged attempt to poison Hitler by injecting gas into the Berlin bunker. While he only "thought" about it, he made the world believe that this was a real attempt on Hitler's life.

He claimed to have done this during the same time frame of his frequent visits to Hitler, in which he pledged his undying allegiance.

During his trial, he made much of his claim that he single-handedly stopped the destruction of what was left of the German industry by circumventing Hitler's "Nero Order", at the risk of his life. This certainly is not true or, at least a wild exaggeration. Kenneth Galbraith, the famous economist, who got to know Speer in 1945, judged that Speer's statements—about his efforts to foil Hitler's destruction orders and other factors—can be seen as a cunning attempt, staged with the composure of a born gambler, to save his own skin and to rise, so to speak, like a phoenix from the ashes.

Instead of ordering the destruction of all factories, railroad stations, post offices and so on, as Speer claimed, the actual order only limited the destruction to military objects or infrastructures that was useful for the advancement of the enemy. Here is a translation of Hitler's actual order of March 19th, 1945:

Teletype M1518/45 g.Rs. dated March 20, 1945 to Reichsminister Speer. The Fuehrer has issued the following order on March 19, 1945:[2]

In reference to: Destructive measures within the territories of the Reich.

The fight for the existence of the German people forces us to use every measure to weaken the fighting forces of our enemy and to hinder his advances, even within the territories of our nation.

Now I therefore order: 1. That all military transport, communications, industry and storage facilities in addition to assets located within the Reich territory, and which can be of use to our enemy in the continuation of their fight against us, either now, or in the foreseeable future, should be destroyed.

Signed: Adolf Hitler – OKW/WEST/Op/Ou 2 Nr. 002711/45, gKds-gez: Winter, Gen-Ltnt u. stellv. Chef West.

It is quite apparent, that this order relates strictly to <u>military objectives that can aid the enemy</u> such as bridges, railroad yards, and ammunition factories, for example. These are measures that any general in the field would take.

Looking at the happenings in the bunker during the last days in April, 1945 I came to the conclusion, that Speer may have been well aware of the arrangement for Hitler's disappearance from the bunker and of the subsequent cover-up.

How else can one explain the clandestine meetings between April 20 and April 22, 1945, with Colonel Baumbach (Hitler's presumed pilot on his trip to Spain) in and around Berlin in addition to the urgent messages between the two? [3] Here is one of the messages from Speer taken from Baumbach's memoirs:

"Dear Winnetou or Knee, it is 4 o'clock on Saturday, the 21st of April (1945) and we are south of Schwerin on the road to Lübesse and waiting until 8 o'clock. If anything happens, Major Strack, Lübeck, Ploennerstr. 8, Tel. 22332 will know. Ask for Colonel Holzhaeuser." (Note the code name "Winnetou" for Baumbach.)

This is highly suspicious. Why would a Minister of the Reich, in a time of great crisis, spend his time meeting secretly with a relatively low-level air force officer?

The second troublesome question is, why did Speer return to the bunker on the evening of April 22nd, at great risk to his life, and stay there till the early morning hours of April 23rd? He claimed that he talked to Hitler (Hitler was gone and the Hitler double was asleep) and to Eva Braun. This is rather disingenuous, certainly Speer, of all people, would have recognized the substitutions.

The only possible reason for taking on this great risk of flying back to Berlin in the evening of April 22nd, 1945, was to give credence to the "make believe" that the real Hitler and the real Eva Braun were still present in the bunker and to check that the cover-up arrangements worked.

It seems clear that Speer risked life and limb out of a deep sense of friendship and loyalty to Hitler.

Here is Speer's background.

Albert Speer was born on March 19th, 1905, the son of a well-to-do architect, and grew up in a large house cared for by a number of servants. After studying in Karlsruhe and in Munich, he moved to Berlin to become the assistant to the well-known architect, H. Tessenow.

Married in 1928, he met Hitler for the first time in 1930

during a lecture in Berlin.

He was impressed and joined the Nazi Party on March 1st, 1931.

A friend, Karl Hanke gave him his first assignment to remodel an office building. He did it well and from there his assignments multiplied and ranged from staging mass rallies to building the new Reich Chancellery in the record time of one year!

This brought him to the attention of Adolf Hitler, who always had a special liking for architecture; indeed his watercolor paintings nearly always featured buildings.

These first meetings developed into what was probably the only personal friendship that Hitler ever nurtured in his later life. This friendship would last till the end of the war.

Speer, as a result, spent a lot of time at the Berghof, Hitler's mountain retreat, where he was seen many times walking with Hitler through the countryside, engaged in long private conversations with the Fuehrer.[4] Speer refused to wear a uniform until he had to, after his appointment as Armaments Minister in 1942, and he kept himself aloof from the other more boisterous party bosses.

He certainly was very intelligent and an excellent organizer. For example, he managed to increase armament production, despite incessant Allied bombing. Such production reached an all-time high in the summer of 1944. Even few days before the end, he drove, together with Major von Posner, all over the country in order to get the production of jet planes going again.

In that sense, he was an ardent supporter of the German war effort, despite his protestations after the war. He was a member of the so-called "radical group" that, together with Hitler, Goebbels, Bormann, Ley, Kaltenbrunner and Saukel, was determined to continue the war in the autumn of 1944.

Notes

1. Joachim Fest, Speer the final verdict, Harcourt, Inc. 1999.
2. Ref; Hermann Historica, Auction April 22,2005. Item: 7508.
3 Werner Baumbach, *Broken Swastika*, Dorset Press, New York, 1960, p. 193.
4., Eva Braun. Home movies from Berchtesgaden.

8 | A VIKING FUNERAL

If, for the sake of discussion, one can assume that the participants in the conspiracy surrounding Hitler's escape wanted to cover his tracks, then one way this could be accomplished was, by pretending that Hitler and Eva Braun committed suicide, assuming the ruse with the double did not work. Well and good, but how about the bodies? Since both disappeared, there could have been no corpses. Here is a way out of this dilemma: you pretend that the corpses were burned beyond recognition, or, had disintegrated into ashes.

While we have no proof that this is what really happened (the conspirators would not admit to it in public), the fact that the Russians could not find corpses of either the real Hitler nor of Eva Braun, gives this explanation more credence.

Anton Joachimsthaler quoted in his book the text of a report, supposedly issued in May 1946, by a high level Russian Task Force formed to investigate Hitler's fate, saying:

Not a trace was found of the bodies of Hitler and Eva Braun. Nor was there any trace of the petrol-drenched grave in which the bodies of Hitler and his companion were allegedly cremated according to a statement by some of the witnesses. Some witnesses have now confessed to swearing an oath to Hitler that, if they were captured, they would claim to have seen Hitler's and Eva Braun's bodies being burned on a pyre in the bunker garden. All the witnesses have now admitted to the investigating committee that they did not see a pyre, nor Hitler's or Eva Braun's bodies.

It has been determined that Hitler attempted to cover his tracks with the help of false witnesses.

HITLER'S ESCAPE

There is irrefutable evidence that a small aeroplane took off from the Tiergarten in the direction of Hamburg. It is known that there were three men and one woman on board. It is also determined that a large submarine left Hamburg harbor before British forces arrived. On board were mysterious people, including one woman.[1]

This makes a lot of sense when looking at the overall evidence. For example, the first part agrees in all essential points with the Nordon Report shown elsewhere.[2] Joachimsthaler[3] agrees that the Russians never found a body of Hitler, burned or otherwise, yet he dismisses all Russian statements by Stalin and other Russian officers that Hitler escaped as being untrue.[4] Why not at least consider the possibility that this could be true?

The question is, why should the Russians lie? What motives would they have? Why not accept that the only three surviving main witnesses to the alleged Viking funeral namely Guensche, Linge, and Kempka, all being fanatical Nazis were lying, as the Russians claimed? To me this seems much more logical.

Concerning the last paragraph of the above report, the Russian generals are surely guessing about the means of Hitler's escape, having no hard evidence to rely upon, in contrast to the physical evidence in the bunker garden. However, it is true that Hanna Reitsch and General Ritter von Greim flew out of Berlin in small planes together with a pilot on April 28th. This would account for the "plane with one woman on board" story by the Russians. The additional agent reports of the submarine departing Hamburg (around April 30) with "mysterious people, including one woman" certainly could indicate that Hitler and Eva Braun-Hitler departed this way (see the chapter titled "The Mysterious Submarines").

Now let's start to analyze the well-reported and most

widely believed story of the funeral, as told by Trevor-Roper and others.

After the suicide the bodies were taken into the garden, just outside the bunker, by Goebbels, Bormann, perhaps Colonel Stumpfegger, and one or two others. Hitler was wrapped in a blanket, presumably because he was bloody. According to Trevor-Roper, the bodies were placed side by side in the garden about three yards from the emergency exit of the bunker and drenched with petrol. Because of the shelling, the party withdrew under the shelter of the emergency exit and a petrol-soaked and lighted rag was thrown on the bodies, which at once caught fire. The burial party then stood at attention, gave the Hitler salute, and retired.

From there on the evidence is more circumstantial. How often the bodies were re-soaked or how long they burned, is not known. One witness was informed that they burned until nothing was left; more probably they were charred until they were unrecognizable, and the bones broken up and probably buried.

Hitler and Eva Braun with "Blondie" and her dog at Berchtesgaden in June of 1942.

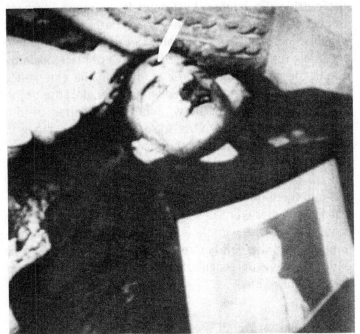

Official Soviet photograph of the Hitler double after death, taken in the Court of Honor of the Reich Chancellery, after exhumation on May 2nd 1945. Note bullet hole in forehead (see arrow).This same photo was published in the 1960s[th] by Russian newspapers with a caption stating that this was the photo of the real Hitler corpse.

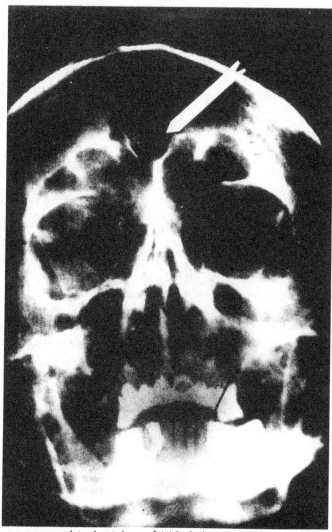

X-ray supposed to be taken of Hitler's head in September 1944. Note circular hole (see arrow) between the two upper sinuses matching the bullet hole in the forehead of Hitler's double. .This fake X-ray photo was later used to identify teeth supposedly belonging to Hitler

Photo taken of the bunker exit to the garden on May 2nd 1945. Note the remaining wood scaffolding and the loose wood planks on the sandy garden grounds showing no signs of a raging fire. The circle marks the spot where Hitler and Eva Braun were supposedly cremated. The observation tower is shown on the right. .A Russian officer is standing inside the emergency exit.

One of the last photographs of the "real" Hitler, showing him smiling and relaxed on April 20th, 1945 while greeting a group of Hitler Youth.

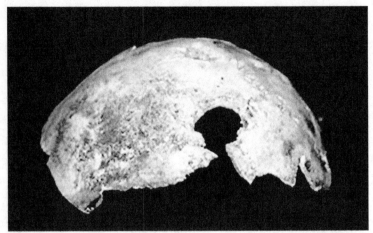

Part of a skull that was unearthed by the Russians in the garden of the Reich Chancellery. It was supposed to belong to Hitler. Note the bullet exit hole in the rear of the cranium, which contradicts the widely accepted theory that Hitler shot himself in the temple. DNA evidence later discovered that the scull belonged to a young woman.

The estate "INVALCO", one of Hitler's presumed residences near Bariloche in Argentina. Photo courtesy of Abel Basti (from: Nazi Bariloche).

Map of Southern Argentina tracing the apparent route taken by Adolf Hitler and Eva Braun during the summer of 1945.

As to the funeral party which carried the bodies into the garden and then burned the bodies of the alleged Adolf Hitler and Eva Braun, there were, according to John Toland[5] and Trevor-Roper:[6] Linge, Goebbels, Bormann, Dr. Stumpfegger, Guensche and Kempka.

From the outset let's remember, that out of these there were only *three* surviving witnesses to this alleged happening: Linge, Kempka, and Guensche. None of the others survived the end in the bunker! So this makes for a very limited verification, especially if each of those witnesses were sworn to plant this particular story.[7] Remember also that the Russian NKVD Commission, the French Police Inspector Gulliaume and others insisted that these three witnesses were lying.

The other trouble with this "officlal" version is the fact that it relies also on hearsay and limited observations from SS guards, who supposedly witnessed the scene from afar but some of whom could not be located later on.[8] I will analyze their testimony later.

Out of the six present at the funeral, only three survived the end of the war and as we know, both Linge and Guensche stated later (after their return from Russia) that they did not see the faces of the corpses. As to Kempka's testimony, he said in 1945 that he was unable to identify the body of Hitler when he helped carry the corpse of a male out of the bunker.[9] "The body was covered by a blanket and I could only see black trousers and black shoes, similar to the ones that are worn by Hitler." This again contradicts his earlier story that he, Kempka, carried *Eva Braun* upstairs. He contradicted himself again by saying first Eva Braun was wearing a black dress, then later on, that she was wearing a blue dress with white trimmings. Similar contradictions appear in the testimony of other witnesses.

For example, Mohnke stated that Eva Braun was covered in a blanket and was wearing no shoes, while Kemka stated there was no blanket, and SS guard Karnau saw Eva Braun's familiar black shoes protruding from under the blanket *after the fire had been burning for ten minutes!*

Anton Joachimsthaler gives the most detailed, recent (1995), and quite well researched account of the funeral in his book, *The Last Days of Hitler.*[10] He quotes Linge as saying:

We placed Hitler's body a short distance from the garden exit of the bunker. Immediately after this Guensche appeared with Eva Braun's body, which we placed next to that of Adolf Hitler. The bodies lay directly next to each other with the <u>*feet*</u> *pointing towards the bunker exit...*

Now contrast this with the testimony of Guensche, who stated:

I want to make it clear that the *heads were pointing in the direction of the bunker exit*, and that – seen from the bunker exit – Eva Braun was lying to Hitler's right.

Of further interest are the statements by Linge, Kempka and Guensche that they did not complete the cremation but left this task to some unnamed underlings. In other words, even though they were supposedly ordered to make sure that no traces remained of Hitler's corpse, they did not bother to check if this was actually done. Very curious indeed! Even Trevor-Roper remarked; "From this moment on no one seems to have given a damn about the past or the two bodies that were still sizzling in the garden."[11] This behavior makes sense only if there were no burned bodies to start with.

As I mentioned before, we have testimony by the

German guards Karnau,[12] Mansfield, and Hofbeck on whose testimony Trevor-Roper heavily relied.

Mansfield said that he observed the burning of two corpses from the observation tower, which was about 45 feet from the cremation site. He further testified that heavy smoke obscured his vision, since a wind was blowing in his direction. His vision was further restricted by a slotted steel window. He stated that cans of gasoline were thrown from the bunker exit and towards the cremation site. From his position and under the given circumstances, we can safely assume that he would not have been able to identify anybody on the ground.

Let's see now what happened with the remains of the supposedly burned corpses.

Here we have Kemka's statement that he buried the remains in the garden and outside the wall of his apartment. Yet this statement was obviously false, since nothing there was found by the Russians. Rattenhuber said that he gave no orders to bury the remains. This leaves only Guensche, who stated that he ordered SS Officer Lindhoff to bury the remains in the garden. Unfortunately, Lindhoff was killed trying to escape from Berlin. We should add to this that one of the SS guards, named Karnau, stated on November 13, 1953 that he saw skeletons of both bodies at around 5 P.M. on April 30, 1945. Yet he corrected his statement on June 30, 1954 by saying, "I did *not* see any bones. What I found was a pile of ashes, which disintegrated when touched by my foot."[13] This makes more sense, and he could have been seeing the remains of the red carpet that was burned and of the destroyed Hitler papers and belongings that were cleaned out of Hitler's rooms and which were burned, that afternoon. As we all know, the remains of burned paper disintegrates when touched.

A similar statement was made by the guard, Hofbeck, who testified that around 8 P.M. there was nothing left to see but flakes of ashes. These statements also agree with Hentschel's testimony that on May 2, he saw no remains in the garden other than the charred bodies of the Goebbels.

We may now look at the cremation itself. Gasoline in liquid form does not burn. Only gasoline vapor does, which requires heat. Since the soil was sandy, we can assume that a major portion of the gasoline disappeared into the ground and thus did not burn at all. Finally, we had testimony that gasoline cans were thrown from the bunker exit towards the corpses (a distance of about three meters or nine feet). We can therefore again assume that a good deal of this liquid got wasted. Since the ground was fairly even and since a wind was blowing, it can further be assumed that a good deal of the flames (creating the heat) were blown sideways and away from the alleged corpses. Gasoline fires can reach temperatures between 1300° and 1500° Fahrenheit, not enough to melt gold[14], for example. Modern gas fired crematoria are much more efficient and can get as hot as 1800° F, partly due to the surrounding walls providing extra heat from radiation, in contrast to an open fire. Yet even here, the bones of a person do not disintegrate into ashes, as Joachimsthaler[15] will have us believe, although extreme heat makes bones brittle.[16] Modern crematoria solve this problem with the remaining bones by grinding them up and by putting the resultant powder in an urn, which is then given to the bereaved.

Aside from the photos of the only partially burned corpses of Joseph and Magda Goebbels, there are quite a few photos published of crematoria in German concentration camps. In almost all of these pictures we see skeletons either still in the oven, or in front of it, despite the fact that these were modern, gas fired devices.

While Joachimsthaler conceded that the Russians did not find Hitler's corpse, he still insists that Hitler committed suicide. His theory was that there was in excess of 200 liters of gasoline burning for over two hours. This is hard to believe reading all the testimony about the extreme difficulty of obtaining gasoline. Then he further theorizes that the shrapnel from the Russian shelling and the use of Napalm made the bones disintegrate into ashes.[17]

The problem with this theory is that Napalm[18] was not used by the Russians in 1945 especially not near the bunker. Furthermore there could not have been much shelling, since the bodies of the Goebbels couple, aside from the burning, showed no sign of damage. Furthermore, there was plenty of wood scaffolding next to the emergency exit and at the observation tower, due to unfinished construction. As photos taken shortly after the fighting show, there was hardly any damage at all to any of these. Even among those planks on the ground, none of those seemed to have burned, despite the alleged raging fire fed by 200 liters of gasoline.

Of course, if the Russians really found two burned corpses somewhere in a shallow grave, then we must accept the story of the funeral as being true unless these corpses came from a burning building (and there were plenty of those). The question only is: since they could not have been Hitler and his wife, who then were those dead persons?

We know for sure that at least two additional persons died from gun shot wounds inside the bunker: General Krebs, and Franz Schaedle. However, neither of those got cremated.

Incidentally, according to Donald McKale, Johannes Hentschel the chief electrician for the Chancellery and the last person to leave the bunker testified that he saw only the charred bodies of Dr and Mrs Goebbels. Of Hitler, Eva Braun, and others from the last days he saw nothing.[19] This agrees with General Müller's story that only Hitler's double, was buried in a shallow grave. This body was truly discovered on May 2, 1945 by Colonel Klimenko, as we see later.[20] However, someone in the bunker decided to bury another corpse made out to look like Martin Bormann. Mueller apparently did not know this, since he left already on April 29. Klimenko too discovered this body, but this did not make the history books.

This brings up the interesting question: what happened to Hitler's double after he was shot (presumably inside the bunker), and who buried him? The fact that we have no testimony concerning this matter could only be explained by a) No interrogator ever asked this important question of the surviving witnesses; or, b) The corpse that bystanders, such as Arthur Axmann, saw being carried upstairs, wrapped in a blanket with the face partly covered, was that of the double, not that of Hitler.

Well, my readers may rightly ask, if the corpse being carried upstairs and later buried in a shallow grave (instead of being burned) was that of Hitler's double, then what happened to Eva Braun? Unfortunately, we have no evidence of what really happened to her.

However, here is a plausible scenario. Remember, the young woman, the "strawberry blonde" (as Dr. Schenck described her) certainly was a substitute for the real Eva, provided by Mueller's security service. Remember, witnesses described that she arrived, together *with* the Goebbels family, at around 6 P.M. on April 22, 1945.[21] From there on she played her part well, staying mostly in the background and seemingly avoiding all social contact with Hitler's double.

In the afternoon of the alleged suicide she probably played dead, for the benefit of all onlookers, and had her limp body carried upstairs by fellow conspirators Bormann, Guensche and Kempka. Once in the garden she most likely ran away to her own private residence. Some bystanders entering the living room afterwards sensed a strong smell of almonds (prussic acid) and therefore thought Eva Braun had poisoned herself. However this smell could have come from the mouth of Hitler's double who, according to SS General Müller, was first poisoned and then shot.[22]

This scenario agrees with the Russian findings.

Notes

[1] Joachimsthaler, Anton, *The Last Days Of Hitler*, Cassell & Co., London, 1995, p. 24.

[2] Brown, Anthony Cave, *The Last Hero, Wild Bill Donovan*, Vintage Books, a division of Random House, 1984.

[3] Joachimsthaler, Anton, *The Last Days Of Hitler*, Cassell & Co., London, 1995, p. 252.

[4] Ibid. p. 252.

[5] Toland , John, *The Last Days*, A Bantam Book/ Randam House, Inc., 1967.

[6] Trevor-Roper, Hugh, *Last Days Of Hitler*, third edition, *The Times*, London, 1946.

[7] Joachimsthaler, Anton, *The Last Days Of Hitler*, Cassell & Co., London, 1995

[8] Douglas, Gregory, *Gestapo Chief, The 1948 Interrogation of Heinrich Mueller*, James Bender Publishing, 1995.

[9] Kempka, Erich, "*Erklärungen von Herrn Erich Kempka vom 20–6–45 und Ergänzende Erklärungen des Herrn Erich Kempka*" vom 4–7–45, given in German to the U.S. investigating officer Harry Palmer.

[10] Joachimsthaler, Anton, *The Last Days Of Hitler*, Cassell & Co., London, 1995, p. 192.

[11] Trevor-Roper, Hugh, *Final Entries 1945 The Diaries Of Joseph Goebbels*, G. P. Putnam's Sons, 1978.

[12] Even Ian Kershaw in his book *Hitler* commented on Hermann Karnau's testimony: "...like a number of witnesses in the bunker, he gave contradictory versions at different times."

[13] Joachimsthaler, Anton, *The Last Days Of Hitler*, Cassell & Co., London, 1995.

[14] Gold has a melting point of 1945° F.

[15] Ibid.

[16] Dix, J. and Calaluce, R., *Forensic Pathology*, CRC Press, LLC, 1998, p. 83.

[17] Joachimsthaler, Anton, *The Last Days Of Hitler*, Cassell & Co., London, 1995.

[18] Napalm, made by Dow Chemical Corp, is made of a mixture of aluminum salt and petroleum jelly. It was widely used in Vietnam.

[19] McKale, Donald M., *Hitler The Survival Myth*, Cooper Square Press, 1981.

[20] Bezemensky, Lev, *The Death Of Adolf Hitler*, Michael Joseph, London, 1968.

[21] The real Eva Braun moved into the Bunker on 4–15–1945 and left, apparently with Hitler on the 22 of April. She was last seen in the bunker around 5 P.M. on that day.

[22] Douglas, Gregory, *Gestapo Chief, The 1948 Interrogation of Heinrich Müller*, James Bender Publishing, 1995.

9 | WHAT THE RUSSIANS DISCOVERED

The Russian generals in Berlin learned of the alleged suicide of the Fuehrer from General Krebs on May 1, 1945, while he was trying to negotiate the surrender of Berlin. When the negotiations failed, Krebs went back to the bunker and killed himself.

Russian female soldiers first entered Hitler's bunker at mid-morning on May 2, 1945, the day Berlin fell, and carried out some looting. In mid-afternoon the first five search teams (reporting to the SMERSH, the Russian Army Counter-Intelligence) arrived led by Lieutenant Colonel Ivan Klimenko.[1]

He soon discovered the Goebbel's charred bodies of the, which he rushed back to his headquarters. Later on, a search team located one body, among others, in an old oak water tank. According to General Mueller, this was an empty, decorative stone pond in front of the new Chancellery. It was used as a temporary morgue for the field hospital located under the Chancellery. The corpse looking like Hitler was actually in a shallow grave next to the pond.

The Russians then used the imprisoned German Admiral Voss to identify this body. He declared that it was that of Adolf Hitler, even though the corpse wore darned socks. When Klimenko returned the next morning, he found the corpse prominently displayed in the main hall of the Reich Chancellery.

There is a widely published photograph of this body showing a hatless person, looking very much like Hitler, with a bullet hole in his forehead. This body was not burnt at all. If it was the real Hitler, then the photo must have been taken inside the bunker, before he was carried out and burnt (as Trevor-Roper later claimed). To add to the confusion, some photos were published in reverse, possibly to misrepresent details. Some pictures show a blurred portrait of Hitler on top of the double's chest. No other photos were ever released by the Russians despite the extreme importance of this forensic investigation.

It is certain that this was the photo of the first Russian discovery and we can safely conclude that this corpse was that of Hitler's double. According to the "Nordon Report" the Russians, too, later identified this corpse as being that of Hitler's double. The Russians later (in the 1960s) even claimed that this photo represented the real Hitler.

It was then ordered that the corpse of the double be cremated, but this process was interrupted on orders from Moscow. The partly cremated corpse was then flown to Russia.

Note: nothing in this official version of events indicated that a second double, that of Martin Bormann, was also found, as indicated in the Nordon[2] Report.

Now comes a widely reported story that made it into the history books, but most likely was a hoax planted by the Russian Military Counter-intelligence Service (SMERSH) to cover up the fact that Hitler disappeared. It is contradicted by the Nordon[3] Report, the statement by SS General Müller[4] and later too contradicted by official Russian publications printed after 1968.

Here goes the story[1] as published only in 1968 (after Stalin's death):

A day went by (it is now May 3, 1945), but by then the Russian team had already decided that they had not found the real Hitler.

The Moscow paper *Pravda* reported on May 3, "Hitler is not in Berlin".

This supposedly caused more frantic searches in the Garden with the result that one Private Churakov climbed into a nearby crater and discovered some legs. After more digging, they unearthed the bodies of a man, a woman and two dogs. Since this seemed not to be what the team was looking for, Klimenko ordered the corpses to be reburied.

Finally on May 5th (probably after more frantic phone calls from headquarters) it clicked: "A man, a woman and dogs"...,that could be Hitler and Eva Braun!

Klimenko went back to the garden and had the bodies dug out again. He then had the badly burned corpses sent to the field hospital in Berlin-Buch. A special team, headed by Dr. Faust Sherovsky, was flown in from Moscow; the bodies were dissected and the first forensic autopsy was performed.

Looking at the partly burned body of the man, they found that the cranium was missing; the man had only one testicle and one seminal cord (Hitler had two). There were no fingerprints since the skin was burned and they discovered glass splinters from a thin-walled ampoule in his mouth. From this, and subsequent chemical analyses of the body tissue, they determined "instant death by cyanide poisoning". There were no bullet holes.

Was this false, since witnesses at that time pointed to death by shooting? The Russian Marshall Sokolovsky was very eager to prove that Hitler was dead, since it would be quite embarrassing for him if the Fuehrer had escaped from under his nose. So he spared no effort in the investigation.

Fortunately, the corpse had some teeth and bridgework left. So they removed the lower jaw and the bridge and started to hunt for Hitler's dentist and his dental records. (Note, these teeth came most likely from the mouth of the double, see chapter titled "The Trouble with the Teeth").

This undertaking proved difficult, since the German SS General Müller had all dental records together with Dr. H. Blaschke, Hitler's dentist, flown out of Berlin.[5]

Incidentally, these records were always kept at the Chancellery and not at Dr. Blaschke's office. Mueller's agents then destroyed the dental records as a precaution.[6] Dr. Blaschke himself was subsequently captured and held by the American Army, but the Russians for some unknown reason refused to request his appearance in Berlin. Blaschke was subsequently asked by his U.S. CIC interrogators to reconstruct Hitler's dental work, but thought he could not do it without his files, which, of course were never found. However Blaschke did give a description of Hitler's teeth[7] and I quote:

Edge to edge bite, 6 upper, 10 lowers only remaining natural teeth. Upper right: 1 Richtman crown, 3, 4, full gold crown, 2&5 dummies. Left: 1 three quarter gold crown, 2 Richtman crown, 3 full gold crown, 4 dummy. Single fixed gold bridge over all uppers. Lower right: 1, 2, 4 normal, 3. 5 full gold crown with lingual bar between. Left: 1 normal, 2 porcelain filling and a pical abscess, 3, 5, 8 full gold crowns, 4, 6, 7 dummies.

General Donovan, on July 28, 1945, sent this information by telegram to the Russian SMERSH General Fitin.[8] However, for some reason, it seems that the Russians never used this vital information. However, this is understandable, if we consider that the Russians simply did not have the real Hitler corpse.

Luckily, the Russians then discovered two dental technicians, Fritz Echtmann and Käthe Heusemann. The Russians also claimed to have found dental records and crown work of Hitler in Blaschke's office, which can not be true, according to Mueller, (see above).

In any case, they asked the technicians to sketch the dental structure "from memory". It should here be noted that apparently, K. Heusemann only helped to treat Hitler once in November of 1944. She was later sent for eleven years to Siberia. This apparently was done to prevent her from publicly contradicting her alleged identification.

So much for the official 1968 Russian version of the "two burned corpses".

By May 15, 1945 the Russian military concluded that this burned corpse truly was that of Hitler. However, Stalin having been told already about two Hitlers (the unburnt "double" and now the new, "burnt" corpse), was still not convinced and told his generals they could be mistaken. As a matter of fact, on May 26, 1945, Stalin told the U.S. envoy Harry Hopkins, in Moscow, "In my opinion Hitler is not dead but is hiding somewhere".[9]

As a result, the Russian Marshal Zhukov held a press conference on June 9, 1945, in which he said, "We could not identify the body of Hitler. I can say nothing definite about his fate. He could have flown away from Berlin at the very last moment." To that, the Russian General Bezarin, added: "He has disappeared somewhere in Europe, perhaps in Spain with Franco. He had the possibility of taking off and getting away." A few days later Zhukov told General Eisenhower privately, that there was "no solid evidence of Hitler's death".

Thus the whole affair began to resolve around the Russian's military desire for "closure" and Marshal Stalin's justifiable suspicion that the military was trying to hoodwink him.

According to Gregory Douglas,[10] *Pravda*, the Soviet Newspaper, on May 13, 1945, said: "Moscow has directed the senior officers of the Red Army in Berlin to discuss nothing about the situation in the Fuehrer bunker."

When Erich Kuby, an editor of the German news magazine *Der Spiegel* (issue No's 9-24, May-June 1965) interviewed the Russian General Boltin, he was told by Boltin in 1960, that as far as he is concerned Hitler's body has still not been found.

On July 17, 1945, at the Potsdam Conference, the Russian leader, Josef Stalin, told U.S. President Harry Truman and U.S. Secretary of State Byrnes over lunch that he thought that Hitler was still alive "in Spain or Argentina". A few days later, he repeated his story to Churchill and to Ernest Bevin, the new Foreign Secretary for Britain.[11] It is quite possible that Stalin got information about Hitler's escape directly from his "mole" inside Hitler's headquarter. Starting in 1942, this mole transmitted all vital German military orders directly to Moscow, typically within twenty-four hours after Hitler issued them. In his book, Louis Kilzer makes a strong case that Martin Bormann was this mole.[12]

Even more revealing is a report written by a Russian high-ranking military commission, originally chaired by Marshal Zhukov (and later by secret service chief Beria) written around May 1946 and supposedly given to the U.S. envoy Harry Hopkins. It reportedly stated:[13]

Not a trace was found of the bodies of Hitler and Eva Braun. Nor was there any trace of the petrol-drenched grave in which the bodies of Hitler and his companion were allegedly cremated according to statements by some of the witnesses. Some witnesses have now confessed to swearing an oath to Hitler that, if they were captured, they would claim to have seen Hitler's and Eva Braun's bodies being burned on a pyre in the Chancellery garden.

All these witnesses have now admitted to the investigating committee that they did not see a pyre, nor Hitler's or Eva Braun's bodies.

It has been determined that Hitler attempted to cover his tracks with the help of witnesses.

There is irrefutable evidence that a small aeroplane took of from the Tiergarten in the direction of Hamburg. It is known that there were three men and one woman aboard. It was also determined that a large submarine left Hamburg harbour before British troops arrived. On board were mysterious people, including a women.

While the first part of this statement, being based on physical evidence and interrogations, seems quite plausible, the last (the means of escape) is certainly guesswork, although a number of small planes left Berlin during the last April days. We know that Ritter von Greim, Müller, von Buelow and a woman, Hanna Reitsch, left this way on April 29th. The submarine escape of Hitler and Eva Braun is more likely

What happened to the burnt corpse of Hitler (probably the corpse of the double) is still bizarre. It was buried in the town of Magdeburg, in an unpaved area at 30–32 Klausenstrasse, then the headquarters of the NKVD. It was later disinterred for another investigation. Finally, in 1970 the Russian Secretary-General Brezhnev agreed to again exhume the remains and have them, this time, completely incinerated and the ashes strewn in the Elbe River near the town of Biederitz (see also Bezymenski's article[14] of 1992). This was done in order to eliminate a possible rallying point for Neo-Nazis.[15] However, there was still no news about the alleged second burnt corpse, namely that of Eva Braun.

The Hitler suicide story again resurfaced in 1968, when Lev Bezymenski, a Russian journalist and member of the KGB, wrote a book,[16] trying to tell the Russian version of the events in the bunker as a counterpoint to the Trevor-Roper story. In his book he stated, citing no supporting evidence, that after dying from poison, Hitler was shot by one of his subordinates (this may well have happened to the Hitler double, whose corpse had a gun shot wound to the forehead and, by that time, had been cremated).[17] He even discussed the cadaver of one of the burnt dogs. Bezymenski identified one as "Blondi", Hitler's favorite. However, the dog that was found had a black pelt with a white under-belly, whereas Hitler's Blondi had a brown pelt. Official Spanish police reports of April 1945 list a "large brown wolfhound" as part of the manifest of Hitler's plane, according to Gregory Douglas.[18] It should be noted here, that there were two additional dogs in the bunker kennel. These two dogs, one belonging to one of Hitler's secretary, C. Christian, were poisoned by SS Sergeant Tarnow, as witnessed by Prof. Haase. The cadavers of those two remaining bunker dogs were later found by the Russians, but not the remains of "Blondi", Hitler's dog!

While Bezymenski stated in his 1968 book[19] that Hitler's body was cremated following the autopsy, and that his ashes were scattered in the winds, he retracted this account and in an article[20] written in 1992 stated that Hitler's corpse had not been burnt but buried and re-buried several times.[21] This again throws doubt on the whole Russian suicide and funeral story.

Cornelius Ryan, the well-known author, visited Moscow in 1963 to find the truth about Hitler's fate. He questioned Field Marshal Sokolovsky among other high-ranking officers. The Marshal told him that the Soviet Union considered Hitler dead. Ryan was further told that the Russians did find a partly burnt body near the bunker. A bullet had entered the right temple and blown out some teeth. Despite the missing teeth, Hitler's dentist then identified the remains as those of the Nazi leader.

This again is very curious and quite contradictory. Now, according to Sokolovsky, Hitler was shot in 1945 instead of being poisoned as originally stated in the 1945 Russian autopsy, and Hitler's dentist (who was at that time in U.S. custody) made the alleged identification.

An editor for the German magazine *Der Spiegel* also tried to pry more information from the Russians and he was able to interview Colonel Klimenko, the first investigating Russian officer to reach the bunker. However, his statements were confusing and still gave no clarification how the Fuehrer died or what the Russians did with his corpse.

All this implies again the likelihood that the official Russian story of two burnt corpses and the alleged autopsy was an elaborate hoax concocted for political reasons.

What shall we make of this? First there is a strong possibility that if a burned body really existed then it could have been another false lead arranged by Müller's security service, using the body of either the General Burgdorf or Colonel Schaedle, both were said to have committed suicide, and neither body was reported to have been found. (SS General Müller[22] stated to his interrogators that General Burgdorf escaped and that he later worked for U.S. Intelligence, a statement to which his interrogator agreed). Finally, this body could have been the corpse of the bogus Bormann who, according to the Nordon Report, had a badly damaged head.[23] Being the "fake" Bormann would lend credence to the Russian report that this male corpse was poisoned and had a missing cranium. Note that this could have been the source of the alleged "Hitler Cranium" on display at the Kremlin. However, more probably, the cranium belonged to the double. The bullet entering his forehead could have dislodged his cranium. As far as poisoning is concerned, all senior members of the bunker entourage had been given capsules with cyanide.[24] Remember, Himmler and Goering died this way too. As to the claimed female body, if it really existed, this could have simply been a German women army auxiliary killed in battle, or it could have been the body of a "fake" Eva Braun.

Finding corpses in the devastated Berlin of May 1945 certainly posed no problems for the Russians.

It is of interest here to note, that SS Major Guensche, a key witness to the alleged cremation, stated to his U.S. CIC interrogators on November 15, 1958, after being released from Russian prisons, "that I did not see the dead Fuehrer". The valet, Linge, and Chief Pilot Baur, gave similar testimony to U.S. investigators after their return from Russian prisons. Both Linge and Baur asked their Russian jailers whether or not they ever found Hitler's body. Both received only evasive answers and were never asked to identify potential corpses.

We have already learned that Hitler's chauffeur, Kempka, did not see Hitler's face either. This is pretty strong and independent corroboration that the supposedly burnt body was never identified as that of Hitler. A West German television program in November 1971 showed X-ray pictures of Hitler purportedly taken by the German Dr. Giesing in September 1944 (in reality an X-ray of the double, see photo). On this program, in which both Dr. Giesing and the former U.S. prosecutor Robert Kempner appeared, it was shown that these photos differed radically from those described in the Russian autopsy report. A steel pin in the lower right incisor is plainly evident. The false teeth in the lower jaw were not attached to the right incisor. There was also a difference in the number of teeth. Both men also reported that Hitler, indeed, had two testicles. This again implies that the Russian "two burnt bodies" story was a fake.

Judge Musmano, after hearing about 200 witnesses in 1948, reached the conclusion that Hitler's corpse was never found.[25]

Highly significant is the report that dealt primarily with the disappearance of Martin Bormann from the bunker, but in which vital clues pertaining to Hitler are revealed.[26] This report was written by Captain Otto. N. Nordon, a special assistant to the U.S. Major General Wm. J. "Wild Bill" Donovan, the head of the OSS, forerunner of the CIA. On May 17, 1945, General Donovan briefly became an assistant to Supreme Court Justice Robert H. Jackson, the U.S. Chief Prosecutor at the Nuremberg War Trials which started in the fall of 1945.[27] Otto N. Nordon had been an attorney in New York before joining the OSS. Donovan thought highly of him and gave him several important assignments in Germany including this report written in Nuremberg and dated November 3, 1945 from which I quote:

Confidential Soviet (Russian) records of their investigative actions reveal the following:

At the time of the capture of the Reich Chancellery during the first week of May 2, through the 8, special teams of Soviet military and police investigators unearthed two bodies from the garden area.

One body was purported to be that of Adolf Hitler and the other that of Martin Bormann.

The Hitler corpse bore strong physical resemblance to Hitler; was dressed in his uniform and had been shot once in his forehead.

The Bormann corpse had a badly disfigured head making identification impossible. It was dressed in an original uniform of Bormann and had authentic papers in his pockets.

Extensive forensic investigations carried out by Soviet experts at the specific orders of Stalin disclosed that the alleged Hitler corpse was that of a younger, shorter double, while the Bormann corpse was that of a larger man. In this case, the uniform coat was made for a smaller man and did not fit the body.

The Hitler body[28] (then) was partially cremated and then, on orders from Stalin, sent to Moscow. The Bormann body was photographed and fully cremated. A study by our experts of both the Soviet reports and the photographs of the remains conclude that neither corpse was authentic.

HITLER'S ESCAPE

The Soviets are now *absolutely convinced* that these bodies were left to provide a *false trail* for investigators. The entire physical area of the Chancellery was probed and excavated by the Soviet specialists *without the discovery of any other bodies or forensic evidence.*

This is very interesting indeed, since it confirms part of the description, regarding the size, given of the Hitler double by SS General Müller. The Nordon Report does not mention later Russian reports that two additional bodies, allegedly of Hitler and Eva Braun, were found on May 5, or six months *prior* to this Nordon Report. This too puts the whole "Viking Funeral" story for April 30 into question. It also supports the Russian leadership's suspicion that Hitler and Eva Braun escaped and furthermore, it confirms the existence of a conspiracy to arrange Hitler's escape and the murder of Hitler's double. What is additionally intriguing is the attempt to fake Bormann's death, in order to wipe out his escape trail too. Note the fact that the Germans did not burn the corpse of the bogus Bormann. This too exposes the whole story of the two partly cremated corpses as a farce.

It can, of course, be argued that the information Captain Nordon received was bogus. Yet vital details fit the overall picture. Remember that Captain Nordon did not get this information through official and open Russian channels but from U.S. CIC Intelligence, the British Secret Service (MI5) and from the confidential files of the Soviet Prosecutor for the International Military Tribunal.

Of added significance is the following statement in the Nordon Report:

U.S. and British agencies have no specific information about the survival or death of Martin Bormann. The Soviets have had and maintain absolute control over both the former Nazi government centers in Berlin and most key witnesses. *They have so far declined any substantive assistance to outside investigation agencies.* [emphasis added]

Coming back to the Russian investigations in May 1945, here their whole effort lacked thoroughness. This is a fact also mentioned and criticized by Trevor-Roper. For example, there is no forensic evidence given of the bunker scene. No bullets or bullet fragments were ever found. Stories were later circulated that bloodstains were found on the sofa in Hitler's study, alas of the wrong blood type. However, some evidence was certainly destroyed since according to the testimony of the German Chief Bunker Technician Hentschel, Hitler's anteroom was set afire by SS Captain Schwägermann, using gasoline. This was done on the orders of SS General Mohnke. This order was carried out during the night from May 1 to May 2. As to the effect of the fire, Hentschel testified that the metal door to the study was red- hot and that the rubber air seals were melting. Later that morning after the anteroom was burnt the first Russians entered the bunker. They were female medical personnel who began immediately to loot the place and later left, brandishing some underwear taken from Eva Braun's bedroom. Later on some officers arrived and apparently discovered the significance of the bunker. These events happened hours before Colonel Klimenko and his investigative team arrived. A lot of evidence may have been tainted or destroyed by this time.

An intriguing question is, why did General Mohnke order Hitler's anteroom to be burnt? The logical answer is, to destroy evidence perhaps of the murder of Hitler's double. One must also remember that Linge had the bloodstained carpet burned.

We may conclude from all of this that there was *no*

positive identification by the Russians of this partly incinerated corpse (if it really ever existed) that was supposed to have been the real Adolf Hitler.

Perhaps the clearest and most truthful statement is the one given by the Russian Marshal Zhukov after he visited the Reich Chancellery on May 3, 1945 and quoted here from Joachimsthaler's book:[29]

After the chancellery had been taken ...we wanted to appraise ourselves on the spot of Hitler's, Goebbels', and other prominent Nazis' suicides. This was difficult, however. No one knew exactly at which place and who had been involved. The statements contradicted each other. Prisoners, mostly wounded, were unsure to say anything about Hitler and his entourage. ...We searched in vain for the pyres where Hitler's and Goebbels[30] bodies had been burned. ... The way the matter stood, I instantly had my doubts that Hitler had committed suicide.

While the Russians did not cooperate in the investigation by the Western Allies into Hitler's death, and did not accept the Trevor-Roper report, they did allow, on December 3, 1945, the Western Allies to dig in the Chancellery garden. This was done a week later, and eight German laborers excavated the grounds. However, all that was found were two hats, one undergarment with Eva Braun's initials, and some documents written by Minister J. Goebbels. When the search team tried to return on the next day, the Russian guards refused entry.

Chief Pilot Baur was beaten mercilessly in Russian prisons for refusing to admit that he flew Hitler out of Berlin and to Spain which, of course, he did not. This again indicates that the Russian Secret Service, then the best in the world, may have had a pretty strong idea of what really happened in Berlin. This comes also across from *Moscow News* of June 2, 1945 saying "Franco Spain War Criminals'

Hideout" and from the Moscow report of the *Los Angeles Times* on April 27, 1945 (note this early date), "Nazis flying to Spanish Island". The Russians undoubtedly received word from their agents in Spain about the possible landing of the German plane on April 27. However without concrete proof, Stalin could not call for an extradition of Hitler. Franco simply would have denied the whole thing. Another reason why the Russian interrogators did not get the whole story about Hitler's flight from the captured bunker crew was according to SS General Müller, that none of the remaining co-conspirators, such as Linge or Rattenhuber, were told of Hitler's final destination after his escape from the bunker.[31] They knew only about his "double" and were sworn to pretend that the real Hitler, together with Eva Braun, committed suicide. This is in line with the "need to know" policy, a standing order issued by Hitler. Besides, this way witnesses could not reveal anything under torture.

Later on, and only after Stalin's death and under Khrushchev's rule in Moscow, did the Russian leadership's attitude towards Hitler change. They now conceded that Hitler killed himself and, in 1960, the *Kazakhstan Pravda* published three photographs, one of them supposedly of the dead Hitler. They quoted I. Y. Sianov, a former member of the investigative team that entered the bunker, as saying: "This is a picture of Hitler's corpse; the hysterical maniac had shot himself at the very last moment. I saw the body.[32] It lay there with a hole in his forehead. His servants had no time to burn the body as he had ordered them to do."

This then is the first Russian denial of their original (1945) story that they found Hitler's corpse and that it had been burned. The published (1960) photo, of course, was that of the unburned corpse of Hitler's double. However, the Russian official policy was, from then on: "Hitler did not escape, he committed suicide" which, after this date was repeated in numerous Russian publications and encyclopedias. It is now an established part of Russian history. With Stalin dead, the Russian generals finally got their way after all!

This "turnaround" by official Russia (by accepting the unburned corpse of the Hitler double as the real thing) finally put the story of the alleged recovery of two burned corpses to rest and, with it, the so called "Viking Funeral" on April 30, 1945 outside the Fuehrer bunker. This was an event, which never happened.

Yet, with all this hoopla, there was still no mention by the Russians of Eva Braun, or of her corpse. This is very curious indeed.

In order to put speculation to an end, a German court in Berchtesgaden issued an official death certificate on Hitler on October 25, 1956, concluding "that Hitler took his own life on April 30, 1945 at 3.30 P.M. in the Fuehrerbunker of the Reich Chancellery in Berlin, by shooting himself in the right temple". Without any evidence, the court then stated that his body, together with the uninjured Eva Braun, were found sitting and lying together on a sofa, by Goebbels, Bormann and others (Goebbels and Bormann, being conveniently dead, would have been unable to make such a statement). It appears that this court adopted the same legal interpretation, later used by U.S. courts in similar cases, namely: if a story has been repeated often enough, it then becomes a historical fact.

A recent book published only in 2005 entitled *The Hitler Book*[33] was written exclusively for J. Stalin to give him insight into Hitler's private life and his assumed ultimate demise. This book was recently translated from the Russian language. In the appendix of the book there is a summary of the Russian investigations into Hitler's death or disappearance. It also repeats what Lev Besymenski , the leading protagonist of the poisoning and "coup de grâce" theories, expounded in his books, published in 1968[1,16] and 1982 (as a counter argument against Trevor-Roper). Remember, Besymenski later recanted in 1996 and admitted that, in his books, he told "deliberate lies".

The "Hitler Book"[33] also exposed the incredible rivalry between the Russian Army Counter-intelligence (SMERSH) and the Russian State Security Apparatus (NKVD). Each was trying to discredit the other when it came to prove Hitler's fate. Stalin deliberately fostered such a rivalry in order to prevent any one secret organization from becoming too powerful and therefore dangerous to him. SMERSH in 1945 was headed by Colonel General Victor S. Abakumov, while the NKVD was lead by Lavrenty Beria. This power struggle lasted till 1951 when Beria managed to put Abakumov in jail.

Here are some highlights from the "Hitler Book":

On the morning of May 5th,1945 units of the Russian Army Counter-intelligence Service (SMERSH) dug two badly burned bodies and two bodies of dogs out of a shallow crater about three meters from the emergency exit of the bunker. *This is not believable since photographs taken on May second of the bunker exit show no crater. In addition, the ground is strewn with wooden planks from scaffolding left over on the bunker buildings.*

The Russians then conducted an autopsy of the two badly burned corpses. The chemical analysis of the body tissues revealed that both were poisoned by prussic acid. The corpses later were identified as those of Adolf Hitler and of Eva Braun, based solely on dental identification by the dentist Dr. Blatschke and the dental technician K. Heusemann, due to lack of any other identification.

The trouble with this story is that Dr. Blaschke, at that time, was in US Army custody in Bavaria and therefore unavailable for the Russians.

This fact alone questions the whole identification. Nevertheless, SMERSH Lt. General Aleksandr A. Vadis (assigned to search for Hitler) informed Stalin on May 27th, 1945, that Hitler committed suicide by swallowing poison.

This whole story did not sit well with Beria, the head of the NKVD, since the German prisoners in his custody, Linge, Guensche and Bauer, insisted that Hitler shot himself.

The Western intelligence services too requested access to the results of the Russian investigation into Hitler's alleged death. The head of SMERSH, Abakumov raised serious objections to giving this report to their Allies. It was clear to him that the Western Allies would immediately spot the weak points in the investigations made by his people. The West at that time believed that Hitler shot himself (see report by Trevor-Roper).

In order to resolve the issue, Beria, the head of the NKVD, then ordered another more thorough investigation of the whole bunker story in December of 1945, under the very fitting code name "Myth". This effort included Lt. Colonel Klausen, Colonel N.F. Osipov and Piotr S. Semenevsky. Of special interest here is the special assignment for the latter two. They were asked to investigate the "disappearance" of Hitler.

This effort then led to the famous re-enactment of the bunker episodes in the spring of 1946, described elsewhere. In addition of checking out the conflicting stories of the German witnesses, Beria also requested another autopsy of the alleged Hitler corpse, which was still in custody of the

Russian Army Counter-intelligence. SMERSH absolutely refused to do this! One only wonders, why?

To finally sway opinion in favor of the "shooting" theory, Beria ordered another digging in the garden of the Chancellery. This yielded two skull fragments (now in Russian archives). Those were promptly declared as belonging to Hitler (without any further identification). The fragments where claimed to belong to Hitler's skull and then were used to show as proof that Hitler shot himself. It was said that the bullet caused the skull to break apart and that was the reason why parts of the skull were subsequently blown out. This claim was made, despite the fact that there was no corroboration by witnesses. The bullet also made an exit hole in the rear portion of the skull, indicating a shot from the forehead instead of through the temple, as the historians claim.

So much for the incredible and unprofessional investigation of Hitler's alleged death.

It is of interest to note, that even though the "Hitler Book" supposedly written in part by Linge and Guensche, it apparently was never read by Stalin. He simply sent it on to the archives, undoubtedly knowing that this book was full of inaccuracies.

This was certainly true, despite the heavy editing that the manuscript underwent. On one page of the last version of the manuscript for the Hitler Book, shown as a facsimile on page 290, there are at least sixteen corrections. To give one example of contradictory statements, on page 273 it is stated that Sergeant Tarnow shot Blondie's (Hitler's dog's) puppies, then Wolf (Eva Braun's dog), Frau Christian's dog and finally his own dog. This makes for more than three adult dogs, yet on page 282 it was stated that the Russians only discovered two dogs and no puppies. Of interest here is that Blondi was not shot at all. This makes sense since Hitler took Blondi with him when he escaped. Now let's discuss the famous skull fragment supposedly belonging to Hitler and residing in the archives of the Kremlin.

First of all, it is only the rear portion of the skull, having a hole through it (most likely the exit hole of a bullet). This piece of bone is lacking any other portions such as teeth, which could be used for identification. As mentioned previously, this fragment was found by the NKVD (Russian secret state police) investigators somewhere in the garden of the Reich Chancellery. There were no other bones or skeletons nearby.

Why the claim was made that this piece of a skull should belong to Hitler is a mystery, since the only way it could be identified as such would be through the analyses of DNA. This was never done. Adding to the mystery is the report by the SMERSH unit (Russian Military Counter-intelligence) who supposedly found two burnt corpses that they alleged were those of Hitler and Eva Braun. This report states that both persons died of poisoning, both had their sculls intact and that there were no bullet holes![34]

Another puzzling aspect of the whole "skull" story is, how a bullet can enter the temple, that is the side of a skull, and then make a right hand turn in the middle of the brain and finally exit through the back of the head? This is reminiscent of the "magic bullet theory" advanced by the Warren Commission. Remember, the consensus among historians (although without proof) is that Hitler shot himself in the temple.

After all this, one can only conclude that there was incredible bungling on the part of the Russian investigators or, more likely, that we have here deliberate falsifications, done for political reasons to cover Hitler's escape from Berlin.

The book *"Who Killed Hitler"*[34] cited a British journalist, Louis C. S. Mansfield who did his own investigation of Hitler's presumed death during the early month of 1946. He concluded:

"The bodies of Adolf Hitler and Eva Braun were NOT burned or cremated in the garden of the Reichchancellory (sic) in Berlin. Careful examination of the exact spot where Hitler's chauffeur, Erich Kempka, said the two bodies had been burned revealed no evidence of any fire".

Notes

[1] Bezymenski, Lev, *The Death Of Adolf Hitler*, Michael Joseph, London, 1968.

[2] Douglas, Gregory, *Gestapo Chief, The 1948 Interrogation of Heinrich Müeller*, James Bender Publishing, 1995.

[3] Ibid.

[4] Brown, Anthony Cave, *The Last Hero, Wild Bill Donovan*, Vintage Books, a division of Random House, 1984.

[5] Douglas, Gregory, *Gestapo Chief, The 1948 Interrogation of Heinrich Mueller*, James Bender Publishing, 1995.

[6] Other witnesses claim that the dental records of Hitler were in the airplane that crashed on the way to Bavaria.

[7] Brown, Anthony Cave, *The Last Hero, Wild Bill Donovan*, Vintage Books, a division of Random House, 1984.

[8] Brown, Anthony Cave, *The Last Hero, Wild Bill Donovan*, Vintage Books, a division of Random House, 1984

[9] Beschloss, Michael, *The Conquerors*, Simon & Schuster, 2002

[10] Douglas, Gregory, *Gestapo Chief, The 1948 Interrogation of Heinrich Mueller*, James Bender Publishing, 1995

[11] Beschloss, Michael, *Dividing The Spoils*, Simon & Schuster, Inc., 2000

[12] Kilzer, Louis, *Hitler's Traitors*, Presido Press, Inc. 2000.

[13] Joachimsthaler, Anton, *The Last Days Of Hitler*, Cassell & Co., London, 1995

[14] *Der Spiegel* a German Newsmagazine, No. 14, 1992, p. 110

[15] Beschloss, Michael, *The Conquerors*, Simon & Schuster, 2002

[16] Bezymenski, Lev, *The Death Of Adolf Hitler*, Michael Joseph, London, 1968

[17] The discovery of poison also agrees with SS General Mueller's testimony that Hitler's double was first poisoned and then shot.

[18] Douglas, Gregory, *Gestapo Chief, The 1948 Interrogation of Heinrich Mueller*, James Bender Publishing, 1995

[19] Bezymenski, Lev, *The Death Of Adolf Hitler*, Michael Joseph, London, 1968

[20] Schellenberger, Walter, *The Labyrinth*, Memoirs, Da Capo Press, 2000

[21] *Der Spiegel* a German Newsmagazine, No. 14, 1992, p. 110

[22] Douglas, Gregory, *Gestapo Chief, The 1948 Interrogation of Heinrich Mueller*, James Bender Publishing, 1995

[23] Brown, Anthony Cave, *The Last Hero, Wild Bill Donovan*, Vintage Books, a division of Random House, 1984

[24] Actually Prussic Acid.

[25] Musmano, Michael, *Ten Days To Die*, second edition, McFadden Books, New York, 1962

[26] Douglas, Gregory, *Gestapo Chief, The 1948 Interrogation of Heinrich Mueller*, James Bender Publishing, 1995

[27] Brown, Anthony Cave, *The Last Hero, Wild Bill Donovan*, Vintage Books, a division of Random House, 1984

[28] The body of Hitler's double.

[29] Joachimsthaler, Anton, *The Last Days Of Hitler*, Cassell & Co., London, 1995

[30] The corpses of the Goebbels had already been removed by Colonel Klimenko on the prior day.

[31] Douglas, Gregory, *Gestapo Chief, The 1948 Interrogation of Heinrich Mueller*, James Bender Publishing, 1995.

[32] The location of the bullet hole in the forehead almost certainly excludes suicide. The double most likely was drugged or poisoned and then got the *coup de grâce* by means of a pistol shot administered by a member of Hitler's security service

[33] The Hitler Book, The Secret Dossier Prepared for Stalin, from the interrogations of Hitler's personal Aides. Public Affairs, New York, 2005.

[34] The Hitler Book,, The Secret dossier Prepared for Stalin, Public Affairs,2005. pp. 28135 Moore, Herbert and Barrett, James, Who Killed Hitler, the Booktab Press, NY, 1947, p. 165.

10 | THE TROUBLE WITH THE TEETH

Any good forensic investigation of a murder, or suicide scene trying to check the victim's identity, includes: looking for fingerprints, checking the victim's blood type, and comparing the dental structures with what is known from previous dental records. Looking at the autopsy report of the alleged Hitler corpse as reported in Bezymenski's book,[1] there could have been no fingerprints since the body was supposedly burned. Nevertheless, one might still be able to extract some bodily fluids in order to establish the blood type. This apparently was not done. Checking for the DNA was of course unknown at that time. This then leaves only the victim's teeth for identification.

Rather than taking the teeth from the supposed Hitler corpse, according to the testimony of the German dental technician K. Heusemann, the Russians removed bridges from the remains of about thirteen to fifteen corpses scattered around the bunker exit.[2] Where did these corpses come from? Surely not from the bunker exit. They came most likely from the stone pond in the Chancellery garden, which was used as a temporary morgue by the German field hospital located near the bunker. Then again we read in Bezymenski's book that the Russian Secret Service took a bridge made of yellow metal and consisting of nine teeth out of Hitler's upper jaw and a single lower jaw containing fifteen teeth out of Hitler's skull.[3]

We know Hitler's dentist Dr. Blaschke was in U.S. custody and all of Hitler's dental records were destroyed.[4] Luckily, the Russians were able to locate two of Dr.

Blaschke's dental technicians. The first one, Käte Heusemann, was arrested on May 9, 1945, in Berlin. Here she was shown a gold bridge with facets that was removed from an upper jaw. She also was shown a complete lower jawbone with teeth and bridges plus an additional bridge made for a lower jaw and consisting of synthetic resin with a gold crown. She immediately was able to identify the upper bridge and the lower jaw with the dental work as those belonging to Hitler. The way she described it, the lower jawbone contained one larger and one smaller gold bridge. One should note here that Dr. Blaschke, Hitler's dentist, in his testimony to his U.S. interrogators mentioned only one lower bridge![5] Further, according to Dr. Blaschke, the upper bridge was fixed. This means it had to be cut from the upper jaw. This is very strange, why was the upper jaw cut but the lower jaw left intact? The reason may be that these parts were recovered from the partially burned corpse of the double.

Hugh Thomas interviewed Käte Heusemann after the war for his book *The Strange Death of Heinrich Himmler*. During this interview, she told him that the Russian Colonel Gorbushin took her to the Dental Station in the Reich Chancellery to help him identify any remaining dental files. No files of Hitler's dental records were found.

Somewhat bizarre is the fact that Frau Heusemann was able to identify a pristine synthetic resin bridge which was also found, as that belonging to Eva Braun. Perhaps she did not realize that Eva Braun's corpse was supposed to have been burned! The bridge could not have come from a cremated corpse, since resin, depending on its type, starts to melt between 300° and 500° F, well below the temperatures reached by a gasoline fire. This leads to the conclusion that the bridge could have only come from Eva Braun's bedroom in the bunker and was therefore useless for the identification of a cremated corpse.

Later on she was shown seven crates partly buried in the earth. These contained the human remains of the Goebbels family, including their children. There was also another crate containing the remains of two dogs.

However, no crates of Hitler or Eva Braun's remains were ever shown to her or to any other German prisoner, despite the fact that L. Bezymenski in his book shows a photo of a box containing some dark matter that was supposedly Hitler's remains.[6]

Later on, K. Heusemann was asked again to identify the same bridge work, this time contained in a cigar box.[7] This she did. One should note here that her description of Hitler's dental works differs substantially from that given by Hitler's dentist, Dr. H. Blaschke, to his U.S. captors. This means that one of the two certainly is lying, or was given the wrong evidence. A similar testimony was given to the Russians by a second dental technician Fritz Echtmann who went essentially through the same interrogation procedure, as did K. Heusemann. Unfortunately, he was briefed by K. Heusemann prior to his arrest. This happened when the Russians released K. Heusemann for a short time after her initial interrogation. Note that in 1944 F. Echtmann was asked by Dr. Blaschke to produce a "skeleton denture" from X-ray pictures of Hitler's teeth. This he did, and one wonders if this bridge work was then implanted into the mouth of Hitler's double,[8] who was first employed as such in the late summer of 1944.[9] This would have been a perfect cover-up, except for the fact that the double was still shorter and his ears did not match. Such an implant again would point to the possibility that the dental items shown to the technicians were taken from the corpse of Hitler's double instead of from the alleged burned corpse of Hitler himself. Since it seems that the X-ray photo of the skull with the bullet hole in the forehead is really that of Hitler's double (see photo), this explains the many inconsistencies in the autopsy report published in 1968 by Bezymenski. But it makes it quite clear that the subject of the autopsy was Hitler's *double* rather than the real Hitler. It also confirms the finding of the U.S. professor of dental biology, Dr. Reidar Sognnaes, that the teeth and bridges used by the Russians for identification matched those shown in the X-ray photo. No wonder they matched, since those teeth and bridges came from the same skull belonging to the "double".

This could explain the "cat and mouse" game played by the Russian Secret Police with the two dental technicians, including their long incarceration in Russia. That the bridges most likely came from the initially unburned double also explains Hitler's unburned and pristine golden Party badge and the Iron Cross medal, which was shown to K. Heusemann for identification. These items certainly could not have come from a charred corpse.

Of great importance here too is the fact that Fritz Echtmann, the second dental technician, was repeatedly questioned (for over one year) by the Russians about the disappearance of Eva Braun, despite the fact that the lower resin bridge was identified as supposedly belonging to Eva Braun's corpse.[10]

Later on in the 1970s, there was also a discussion of X-ray pictures of Hitler's head, which supposedly were used to identify the teeth and bridge work, but were reported to have "proved too meager" for diagnosis. Copies of some of these films are at the U.S. National Archives; but none of these have the standard German military and medical information on them.[11] Again, the simple explanation is that these films were made by the Russians depicting the head of Hitler's double. In 1972 Dr. Reidar Sognnaes, a professor of dental biology in California, believed that he was now able to positively identify Hitler's dental work using the above films and by comparing them to the illustrations in L. Bezymenski's' book (showing the X-ray photo of the skull of the double). This identification was obviously correct; the teeth taken out of the skull of the dead double did match the teeth shown in the X-ray photo of the double's head. No surprise here!

However, Sognnaes concluded that the burned female corpse allegedly found was *definitely not* Eva Braun!

As mentioned previously, part of the so-called evidence of Hitler's identification through his dental works came from an X-ray photo that was supposedly taken by Dr. Giesing on September 19, 1944. This film was found in the U.S. archives but as mentioned showed none of the typical German markings and dates. What is startling is that this photo clearly shows a neat circular hole in the forehead and between both frontal sinuses, slightly to the left of the center of the head. This hole corresponds exactly with the bullet hole in the forehead of Hitler's double. This then is no doubt an X-ray photo taken by the Russians of the head of Hitler's double's after he was disinterred on May 2, 1945. A copy of this photo might then have been given to U.S. Intelligence as a photo of Hitler's head (perhaps before the true identity of the double was discovered). This, too then puts the whole dental identification into the realm of political fiction.

Notes

[1] *Der Spiegel* a German news magazine, No. 14, 1992, p. 110.

[2] Joachimsthaler, Anton, *The Last Days Of Hitler*, Cassell & Co., London, 1995.

[3] Bezymenski, Lev, *The Death Of Adolf Hitler*, Michael Joseph, London, 1968.

[4] Douglas, Gregory, *Gestapo Chief, The 1948 Interrogation of Heinrich Müller*, James Bender Publishing, 1995.

[5] Brown, Anthony Cave, *The Last Hero, Wild Bill Donovan*, Vintage Books, a division of Random House, 1984.

[6] Bezymenski, Lev, *The Death Of Adolf Hitler*, Michael Joseph, London, 1968.

[7] It was reported that she selected Hitler's bridge from many others in that box. This was not true according to her testimony.

[8] Some of us may have seen a movie in which a gangster, trying to disappear, had copies of his teeth implanted into a handy corpse, which then was burned in a fake auto accident. The police then promptly identified the corpse as that of the gangster and declared the gangster as dead.

[9] Douglas, Gregory, *Gestapo Chief, The 1948 Interrogation of Heinrich Müller*, James Bender Publishing, 1995.

[10] One can assume that this was a removable bridge that was simply forgotten by Eva Braun in the bunker while she escaped with Hitler.

[11] Douglas, Gregory, *Gestapo Chief, The 1948 Interrogation of Heinrich Müller*, James Bender Publishing, 1995.

11 | WHATEVER HAPPENED TO HERR SILLIP, HITLER'S DOUBLE?

Now let's see what might have actually happened to the poor Herr Sillip, which seemed to be his name according to General H. Müller[1], after he was forced or talked into playing Hitler's double. The following story is based on the most credible of the multiple witness testimony, including that of Müller's, and on the latest Russian sources[2]. Part of the account is pure speculation on my part. Unfortunately, nobody will ever know the complete facts in this matter.

As we already know from Heinrich Müller's statement, Hitler together with his dog "Blondi" supposedly walked out of the bunker on Sunday, April 22nd, around 8 p.m. and then disappeared[3]. Eva Braun also left shortly after 5 p.m. on the same day[4]. We also know that before leaving the bunker, Hitler telephoned Dr. J. Goebbels to come and move with his family into the bunker[5]. This command must have come somewhat sudden since Goebbels, being in a hurry, forgot to bring extra shirts[6]. In any case the family arrived around 6 PM bringing with them a young lady[7], who from then on pretended to be Eva Braun. She dressed and wore her hair to suit the part. Her accent was not quite the same as Eva's, but then again very few people ever met the real Eva Braun. Besides, she later kept much to herself in the bunker and seldom joined the double at meal times[8]. Unlike the real Eva Braun, she started smoking in the bunker.

Dr. Goebbels, having said goodbye to Hitler, settled down in his new abode. Hitler's double then arrived at the bunker shortly after 8:30 p.m. accompanied by Linge,

Kammhuber and a German shepherd dog[9]. The pair showed the double to his rooms and introduced him to the new Eva Braun. After an initial meeting and briefing by Dr. Geobbels, who was to be his mentor from now on, the new Hitler had dinner and tried to sleep, being unaccustomed to the noise from the ventilation system and the stale smell of the bunker air. It felt strange to him, to lie in the same bed that his admired leader occupied just a day earlier. His mind drifted off and he remembered his uneventful life in Breslau[10,11] without all this excitement and worries. He finally dozed off. It had been an exciting and exhausting day for him.

It started routinely enough, but then in the afternoon, he was visited by General Kammhuber, the head of Hitler's bodyguards. He came to his apartment at the Kaiserhof Hotel,[12] telling him the important date, for which he had been trained for, had arrived. Herr Sillip was glad that the seemingly endless wait was over. Yet he was nervous and apprehensive. How well would he perform and, more importantly, what would be his ultimate fate? Having no alternative, he dressed carefully in a brand new uniform, exactly matching that of Hitler's. Kammhuber reminded him to put on the special platform shoes (to make up the difference in height)[13] and to pin on the Iron Cross medal, plus the golden Party badge. Finally, having donned a gray overcoat and the correct cap, he was ready to leave through a back entrance and into the waiting car. It was now dark and a chilly wind was blowing. A distant grumbling reminded them that the Russian artillery was getting closer.

They were now driven through the rubble strewn streets to the rear of the Reich Chancellery garden. Here they were met by a guard who brought with him a German shepherd dog. It had a black and white pelt (instead of the yellow and black pelt of Hitler's dog)[14] but which otherwise looked identical. It was hoped that the difference might not be noticed in the dim bunker light. During their wait, Kammhuber told the double again about the importance of his mission. He had to be here in order to let the world know that Hitler was still in Berlin. This would strengthen the morale of the Berliners and would stiffen the resistance of the German forces against the onslaught of the Red Army. In the meantime, Hitler would secretly go to Bavaria to organize a relief army in order to rescue Berlin.

Finally, after waiting for about one hour at the garden entrance in the chilly evening air, and hoping for no air raid, the pair noticed the approach of Adolf Hitler, accompanied by his dog, Blondi, and his valet Heinz Linge, the latter carrying a flashlight whose light danced eerily on the grassy path. Hitler greeted his double and wished him "good luck" and then turned to Linge thanking him for the many years of loyal service and reminding him of his loyalty oath and to never let anybody know what happened here. Hitler then walked towards a waiting helicopter and disappeared forever. Kammhuber now motioned to the double that it was time to go, and all three men (Linge included) walked towards the bunker exit, meeting on the way General Heinrich Müller who was watching the small group with obvious satisfaction. He was happy; all was going according to plan so far.[15]

The next day the new "Hitler" awoke around 8.30 a.m. and had his breakfast. The same day, Martin Bormann intercepted a teletype from Hermann Goering requesting to be put in charge if he did not hear from Hitler. This posed a dilemma for Bormann, since now there was no real Hitler present. He therefore ordered Goering to be arrested for treason, in the name of Adolf Hitler (without of course consulting the poor double).[16] As part of his new duties, Herr Sillip had to attend a noon military conference dealing with the battle of Berlin. Of course, here he could contribute very little. Luckily, Dr. Goebbels did most of the talking[17]. Nevertheless, there were many hours spent by Dr. Goebbels instructing the double in what to say in order to prevent any slip-ups. Then lunch. The food was not to his liking, as he was not used to vegetarian meals, consisting mainly of soup or spaghetti. Unfortunately, the spaghetti sauce sometimes found its way onto the double's tunic, as noticed by Dr. Schenck[18]. This proved embarrassing to Linge, since he forgot to bring a second uniform for the double. After lunch another military briefing, otherwise waiting many boring hours. This pattern was repeated for the next days. On this first day Albert Speer, Hitler's Armaments Minister and confidant, arrived late in the evening in order to see if everything was going well[19]. Unfortunately, the new Hitler was already asleep, not yet being used to late hours. Speer spoke instead to Magda Goebbels, Dr. Goebbel's wife, and also talked to the "new" Eva Braun. Speer departed early in the morning. He left the bunker for the last time, being satisfied that the plan was working, although he noticed a troubling lack of discipline. In addition, he noted with disdain that the bunker interior looked untidy, with half-empty liquor bottles standing around, a drastic change in appearance from just the day before!

The double now started to spend more time with Professor Haase, who was assigned as his physician and who administered daily injections of supposed vitamins, in reality these were tranquilizers in order to keep the double docile and content. During one of his meetings with Dr. Goebbels, the double was told that arrangements were made to assure his escape. Somewhat annoying was the fact that nobody around him showed him much respect. For example, the officers did not bother to stand up and salute when he entered the conference room. Also, nobody bothered to take a picture of him, unlike the real Hitler, who always had some photographer hanging around him. Finally, people started to smoke in his presence, a practice that Hitler never tolerated.[20] This made him think, do they suspect that I am only a double?

It was a welcome interruption to the routine, when on the evening of April 26th, his fourth day in the bunker; the double was visited by General Ritter von Greim and his pilot Hanna Reitsch[21]. He recognized Hanna from her many publicity photos and he enjoyed her spirit and had a jovial conversation. She might have recognized the Hitler substitution. However, even if she did, she did not let on, being one of the most loyal and dedicated followers of Adolf Hitler. Goebbels asked the double to promote the General to the rank of Field Marshal and appoint him as the new head of the Luftwaffe. This he did gladly, feeling sorry for the badly wounded fellow.[22]

On Saturday, April 28th; Goebbels drew the double aside and said, "The Russians are getting closer and it is time to prepare our escape. However, Adolf Hitler had one final wish: he wanted the world to know that he loved his companion Eva Braun and that he considered her his wife. It is therefore arranged to have a formal wedding ceremony in order to make this marriage official. Now, you have to play the bridegroom, since the real Hitler can not be here. However, all you have to do is say yes when asked. The marriage certificate is already signed, so you don't have to bother with that. Afterwards, we are all going to have a little party."

It was around midnight when the notary, a *Herr* Wagner[22] finally arrived for the ceremony. The small group, Wagner, the double, the "new" Eva Braun, Dr. Goebbels and Martin Bormann were all ushered into the small conference room. The latter two gentlemen were to serve as witnesses to the proceeding. After a small speech, the notary asked the bride and groom if they wanted to be married. The answer was yes. The ceremony ended after the notary and the two witnesses signed the marriage document. The bride and the groom felt somewhat silly, akin to schoolchildren playing "let's pretend". Herr Sillip was glad that he did not have to kiss his new "wife". The wedding party then joined a small group of staffers for a small party in Hitler's study drinking champagne and eating sandwiches. In attendance were: the two secretaries, Junge and Christian, Dr. Neumann (Goebbels' assistant), Walter Hevel, General Krebs, and General Burgdorf[23]. Other people drifted in and out. Both Goebbels and Bormann excused themselves, Goebbels wanting to write his testament. Then to bed. It was already past midnight, and again, it had been a long day for the double.

On the next evening, on Sunday April 29th , after supper with Dr. Goebbels, Martin Bormann and *Frau* Goebbels (note again absence of the new "*Frau Hitler*")[25,26] Dr. Goebbels gave the double sheets of paper. He requested that the double should use Traudl Junge to dictate a will. Obeying Goebbels' wishes, he called Junge into his conference room and began the dictation.[27] This puzzled Ms Junge since she had to use shorthand. The normal procedure used by the real Hitler was to dictate from memory directly into the typewriter. Also strange was that the double failed to proof-read the typed manuscript. Hitler would never let a typed document leave his office without thoroughly reading and correcting it[28]. Judging by her memoirs,[29] she never discovered the true identity of what she thought was her Fuehrer. General Heinrich Müller, whom she met during the last bunker days, characterized her as very young (she just turned 25) and naïve. Yet, she must have had her nagging doubts concerning her boss. There seemed to be something odd about him. Again, any doubts she might have had were dispelled by the attitude of others around her, especially by the behavior of Dr. Goebbels, who, of all people, should know. Up to the end, he treated her boss with respect and always addressed him as "*Mein Führer*".

The night of April 29 also turned out to be a long one and the double was not feeling well. Professor Haase therefore asks Dr. Schenk, who was operating on wounded soldiers in the cellars of the Reich Chancellery, for consultation[30]. When Schenk arrived he was shocked to see the run-down condition of what he thought was the real Hitler. He also wondered about the soiled uniform. He never had seen Hitler closeup before.

It was now Monday, April 30th and the Russians could be entering the bunker at any time. After lunch, Rattenhuber informed the double that the time has come to leave the bunker and to say goodbye to the staff. These were awkward and perfunctory handshakes for the small group of bunker survivors assembled in the narrow hallway[31]. It only lasted for about three minutes. He was joined by his new bride for the occasion, having so far avoided contact with her. It was now 3 p.m. and the couple was ushered into their living quarters where Prof. Haase and General Rattenhuber were waiting. Rattenhuber had already instructed Guensche, brandishing a machine pistol, to guard the door and to let nobody enter[32]. Prof. Haase now proceeded to give Hitler his customary "vitamin" shot, while the new "Eva" went to her bedroom. This time, the solution injected was different and caused the double to lose consciousness. Then Prof. Haase inserted a capsule of cyanide (actually a prussic acid compound) into the double's mouth and compressed his jaws trying to break the glass capsule, while the double still was sitting on the sofa. Haase had tried the poison on the two remaining dogs (one belonging to Frau Christian, the other to Sergeant Tarnow, the dog handler). The poison normally worked quite fast, except in this case some of the poison may have run out of the mouth of the double and he convulsed.

To illustrate what can happen when someone has swallowed or breathed cyanide, the following is a description by the British Dr. Wells, who witnessed the suicide of the SS- Chief Heinrich Himmler on May 23rd, 1945, while in British custody, as reported in the book The Strange Death of Heinrich Himmler, *by Hugh Thomas, on page 165: "He crushed the glass capsule between his teeth and took a deep inhalation. His face immediately became deeply suffused and contorted with pain. His neck veins stood out and his eyes stare glassily, and he crashed to the ground. There was a slowing series of torturous breaths, which may have continued for half a minute, and the pulse for another minute after that."*

Rattenhuber then decided to end the agony of the double and, to assure his death, by taking a 7.65 mm caliber pistol and by shooting the double in the forehead. Unfortunately, this caused a perforation of the double's cranium and, as a result, there was considerable bleeding. Some blood splattered onto the wall behind the sofa[33]. Rattenhuber now called "Frau Hitler" from her bedroom and asked her to sit on the sofa and pretend to be dead. It is unlikely that she poisoned herself, since there was only one empty poison vial found on the end table next to the sofa. This poison was used for the double (one may note that the Russians found parts of the glass vial still in the double's mouth). Yet, with the strong smell of almonds in the room, people entering the room would assume that Eva Braun-Hitler had poisoned herself. The young lady playing Eva

Hitler-Braun was no doubt an accomplished actress, hand picked by Dr. Goebbels who was in charge of all cultural activities, including theaters and the movies. After all, one of the scenes taught in a *Schauspielschule* is to play dead on stage. Goebbels was quite a ladies man especially with aspiring actresses. He was quite charming, and according to one of his secretaries he had "quite an enchanting smile and very sexy eyes". It must have been easy for him to convince one of the young actresses to play the role of "Eva".

The two men now left the apartment, having finished their task, instructing Guensche to wait another ten minutes before letting anyone enter.

Rattenhuber did not feel well after his deed and consumed a few glasses of cognac in order to steady his nerves.

By now word had spread among the top echelon that Hitler committed suicide and a small group started gartering at the door to Hitler's rooms. Guensche, guarding the door, kept checking his watch; ten minutes seemed like an eternity.[34] He finally opened the door and Linge rushed in and noticed the pistol on the floor (this tends to speak against a suicide, since the victim typically clutches the gun in his hand). He quickly left the room again; the smell of the cyanide gas was too strong for him[35]. Finally, after some minutes Goebbels, Linge and Guensche entered the room and observed the scene. Guensche then ordered to have the corpse of the double laid down on the rug which covered the floor of the living room. Laying down the body caused more bleeding from the rear of the double's head onto the rug, staining a large round area about ten inches in diameter. Soon afterwards Linge had the rug burnt since it was soaked with blood [36]. Still, some blood seeped through the rug and left a large round discoloration on the floor[37]. Now Guensche ordered some of the guards to come in and wrap the two bodies in blankets. Then both were carried upstairs through the narrow staircase and through the emergency exit into the garden, where they were laid out on the ground. Kempka, who carried the assumed Eva Hitler-Braun up-stairs, testified that her body felt limp. This could have been an indication that she was alive[38]. In addition, all witnesses said, that in contrast to the corpse of "Hitler", Eva's body was not covered. Also, nobody bothered to check whether Eva Hitler-Brown was dead or alive.

One must note here that Guensche gave strict orders, prior to the carrying up of the pair, that all guards in the vicinity of the exit were to be removed, thus eliminating any witnesses able to observe what might happen to the alleged Hitler's corpse. The funeral cortège, having done their work, went back into the bunker. Now the rest of the personnel in the bunker were told that Hitler and his wife had committed suicide. It all sounded so plausible, even to the present generation.

It was a perfect crime.

Having been left alone in the garden, the young actress took the opportunity to get up and leave the garden. Sometime later, Guensche ordered the double to be buried in a shallow grave next to a decorative stone pond. Later, on the afternoon of May 2nd, the Russians promptly discovered the corpse, following some digging. Yet, there was no peace for the poor Herr Sillip. Having been dug up, he was prominently displayed and photographed in the courtyard of the Reich Chancellery. The Russians were convinced that this was the real Hitler; after all, he was identified as such by the German Admiral Voss. This is a testament to the close resemblance of the double to Hitler. Here we have a close associate of Hitler, who, even though he attended many military conferences with the real Hitler, was misled by the double's appearance. On May 5th, the Russians became suspicious that they had been hoodwinked and that they could have a double on their hands. They found that the corpse wore platform shoes to hide the lack in height; also his ears did not quite match. Finally, he wore darned socks and had only one testicle.

Colonel Klimenko now had the double brought to his headquarters. He learned from his superiors that his supreme leader, Josef Stalin, knew that Hitler was not in Berlin. As a matter of fact, he was informed that Hitler had escaped. It was therefore decided to have the corpse of the double incinerated, it being no longer of any use. While the incineration was in progress, an urgent phone call was received from Moscow ordering to save the corpse. This seemed silly to Klimenko, but orders are orders!

So whatever remained of the double was packed in ice and flown to Moscow for further tests, including the taking of X-rays of the corpse's head (see attached photo). Just to make sure this was not the real Hitler. Still later the remains served as a prop in the 1968 fake autopsy report written by Lev Bezymenski[44].

Some time, after Stalin's death, the remains were shipped back to Germany and interred in the courtyard of the NKVD (Russian Secret State Police) headquarters in the town of Magdeburg, then in the Russian Zone of Occupation.

Finally, in 1970 the poor fellow or what remained of him was again dug out and completely incinerated. The ashes were strewn into the Elbe River. His tortured soul was finally at peace, or so we hope.

NOTES

1. Douglas, Gregory, *Gestapo Chief, The 1948 Interrogation of Heinrich Müller*, James Bender Publishing, 1995.
2. *The Hitler Book*, The Secret Dossier prepared for Stalin, Public Affairs, New York, 2005.
3. Douglas, Gregory, *Gestapo Chief, The 1948 Interrogation of Heinrich Müller*, James Bender Publishing, 1995, p.191.
4. O'Donnell, James, *The Bunker*, Da Capo Press, 1978, p.114.
5. Ibid., p. 115.
6. Ibid., p. 118.
7. Ibid. , p.118.
8. Toland, John, *The Last Days*, A Bantam Book/Random House, Inc., 1967 , p.591.
9. Douglas, Gregory, *Gestapo Chief, The 1948 Interrogation of Heinrich Müller*, James Bender Publishing, 1995, p193.
10. Joachimsthaler, Anton, *The Last Days Of Hitler*, Cassell & Co., London. 1995, p. 257.
11. Douglas, Gregory, *Gestapo Chief, The 1948 Interrogation of Heinrich Müller*, James Bender Publishing, 1995, p.193.
12. Ibid., P.194.
13. Ibid. ,P.194.
14. Ibid. ,p.215.
15. Ibid. ,p.192 .
16. O'Donnell, James, *The Bunker*, Da Capo Press, 1978, p. 130.
17. *HITLER'S GENERALS, Military Conferences* 1942-1945, enigma books, New York , 1962.
18. O'Donnell, James, *The Bunker*, Da Capo Press, 1978, p. 159.
19. Fest, Joachim C., *Inside Hitler's Bunker*, Picador, Farrar, Straus and Giroux, NY, 2002, p. 74.
20. Junge, Traudl, Until the Final Hour-Hitler's last secretary, Arcade Publishing Co. 2003, p. 182.
21 Joachimsthaler, Anton, *The Last Days Of Hitler*, Cassell & Co., London. 1995, p. 117.
22. *The Hitler Book*, The Secret Dossier prepared for Stalin, Public Affairs, 2005, p. 812 .
23. Joachimsthaler, Anton, *The Last Days Of Hitler*, Cassell & Co., London. 1995, p. 128.
24. Fest, Joachim C., *Inside Hitler's Bunker*, Picador, Farrar, Straus and Giroux, NY, 2002, p.101.
25. O'Donnell, James, *The Bunker*, Da Capo Press, 1978, p.221.
26. Joachimsthaler, Anton, *The Last Days Of Hitler*, Cassell & Co., London. 1995, p. 150.
27. Ibid., p. 129.

28. Junge, Traudl, Until the Final Hour-Hitler's last secretary, Arcade Publishing, 2003, P. 183.

29. Joachimsthaler, Anton, *The Last Days Of Hitler*, Cassell & Co, London. 1995, p. 129.

30. O'Donnell, James, *The Bunker*, Da Capo Press, 1978, p 158.

31. Ibid., p. 222.

32. Ibid. ,p. 223.

33. Joachimsthaler, Anton, *The Last Days Of Hitler*, Cassell & Co., Arcade Publishing Co. 2003, p.155.

34. O'Donnell, James, *The Bunker*, Da Capo Press, 1978, p 225.

35. Ibid., p.233.

36. Joachimsthaler, Anton, *The Last Days Of Hitler*, Cassell & Co., Arcade Publishing Co. 2003, p.162.

37. Ibid., p. 156.

38. Moore, Herbert & Barrett, James, *WHO KILLED HITLER*, The Booktab Press, NY. P.109.

39. *The Hitler Book*, The Secret Dossier prepared for Stalin, Public Affairs, New York, 2005, p 281.

40. Fest, Joachim C., *Inside Hitler's Bunker*, Picador, Farrar, Staus and Giroux, NY, 2002, p 159.

41. O'Donnell, James, *The Bunker*, Da Capo Press, 1978, p.366

42. Ibid. p. 161.

43. *DER SPIEGEL*, a German news magazine, Number 14, 1995, p.110.

44. Bezemensky, Lev, *The Death Of Adolf Hitler*, Michael Joseph, London, 1968.

12 | RUSSIAN INTERROGATIONS

While Stalin's public statements insisting that Hitler escaped could be dismissed as politically motivated, or as "personal prejudice", as some historians claim,[1] no such motives could apply to the NKVD officers who questioned (and tortured) the German bunker survivors for years in Russian prisons without being burdened by "cold war" considerations.

Of special interest to us is the fact that the major questions of the interrogators always revolve around two topics: first, any information about Hitler's double, and secondly, the facts surrounding Hitler's escape. Such repeated questioning within the secret confines of the notorious Lubyanka prison in Moscow, for example, must have been based on more than mere suspicion.

These secret police officers rightfully questioned the official Western suicide story because they had found no corpse of either Hitler or Eva Braun. The Russian Secret Service also concluded that it was not logical to have, within the limited confinements of the bunker and its garden, a double suicide, without finding the two corpses (or at least some remains), a fact that is conveniently ignored in the literature. Gasoline, especially in an open fire, does not generate sufficient heat to completely incinerate all human remains. The body of Dr. Goebbels was still recognizable despite the raging fire. In any case, the bones would still be present.

One can safely assume that someone in Hitler's entourage, probably the famous Russian mole, informed Stalin of Hitler's escape[2] on April 22, 1945 and his subsequent replacement by a double. Stalin then most likely passed this information on to his Secret State Police.

During the long interrogations of the surviving bunker Nazis, interspersed by torture[3], at least one of the prisoners broke and admitted that everyone had sworn to pretend that Hitler and Eva Braun committed suicide in order to cover Hitler's tracks. [4]This of course confirmed the suspicion of the Russian Secret Police (and Stalin's belief) that the pair had escaped from Berlin. This breakdown and the confession of some of the prisoners, were most likely the result of Rattenhuber's admission, in a Moscow prison, that Hitler (undoubtedly meaning Hitler's double) was poisoned and then shot. As Guensche later stated, "Rattenhuber got us in to a lot of trouble."

Nevertheless, when these prisoners were finally released in the 1950s to West Germany they maintained their cover story. Why was this? Well, by then the West firmly believed in the suicide story promoted by Trevor-Roper and others. Thus the former prisoners such as Linge, Guensche, and others, were encouraged to stick to their story by their British and American Intelligence debriefers. To admit that the Russians may have been right all along would have been politically impossible at a time when the Korean War was raging and the cold war was at its most intense.

This then is the supreme irony of the whole story.

Here is an example of the Russians' concern about Hitler's flight to Spain that Stalin and his secret police already knew about. There are statements by Hitler's chief pilot, Hans Bauer, given in November 1955 after his release from Russian prisons: [5]

"During the winter of 1945/46 and in the spring of 1946 I was interrogated in Lubyanka prison[3] time and time again, mainly by Commissar Dr. Savieliev. During these interrogations, I was accused time and time again of flying Hitler out of Berlin."

Baur was continually beaten on the head since the Russians did not believe his denials. Again he stated, "I always was accused of flying Hitler out of Berlin." Bauer finally went on a hunger strike, in order to put an end to his ordeal.[3]

Heinz Linge, Hitler's valet was questioned in the same vein:

"After I was captured on the evening of May 1, 1945, I was questioned by various officers and then taken to Moscow in December of 1945. I was held in Lubyanka prison and then transferred to the Butyka prison. Here I was questioned for about two and a half weeks, always at night.[4]

The subject of these interrogations was always the question, was Hitler dead or alive? The talk always was about whether he (Hitler) was flown out. There was also constant talk whether a double had been substituted. I was always required to describe my experience in connection with Hitler's suicide in detail. During the interrogations I was always maltreated."[8]

Finally, he said that when he was temporarily transferred back to Berlin in April of 1946,[9] his Russian captors asked him about Hitler's measurements. This is intriguing, since we know that the double was about two inches shorter. This last interrogation happened shortly before the Russian Commission issued their concluding report in May of 1946, stating that there was no corpse of Hitler and that the witnesses were lying. Linge then mentioned that he had a cell-mate named Ackermann who told him that Hitler and Eva Braun both took poison and that Hitler was then shot (this probably referred to the fate of Hitler's double).

Now we come to the 1955 statements by Hans Hofbeck, another Russian prisoner and former SS guard. Among other things he stated:

"The interrogators in Moscow kept harping on the question, who was Hitler's double? Who shot the double? Who brought Hitler out (of Berlin)?"

He then said:

"I answered the question about the double by saying there had been a porter in the Chancellery who had borne a resemblance to Hitler. This man had facial features that resembled Hitler's and also a similar moustache and a similar hairstyle. However, he was a little shorter. Otherwise I kept insisting that Hitler was dead and that a double had not been shot and burned in his place."

(The last part was certainly true; the Germans did not burn the double).

During later interrogations (probably part of the famous re-enactment of the bunker episode, in April 1946) he shared a cell with Chief Pilot Baur. Here Baur mentioned to him, "A long time ago, a man from Breslau had been presented who looked very much like Hitler. However, Hitler strictly refused."[5][10]

Otto Guensche, another bunker survivor was captured on May 2, 1945 and he too was flown to Moscow. Here he was accused of lying when he stated that Hitler killed himself. At one point they even told him that he let himself be captured on purposed in order to mislead the Russians and to create a false trail.[6]

Here is part of the testimony of the bunker technician Hentschel,

"The interrogations took part mainly at night. During these I was badly mistreated several times. During one of the beatings, my right eardrum was ruptured. I was told that Hitler was still alive... The claim was made that someone else was cremated....[11]

It is clear from these questions of the Russian interrogators that they knew that Hitler flew out of Berlin. What they did not know (and which the captured Nazis did not know themselves) was, where did he go and who was the pilot? It is equally apparent that they knew about Hitler's double, except that they lacked details about who he was and where he was from. It would certainly be illogical to ask these questions if you already had an identified Hitler corpse, as it was claimed later.

One must admit that it was is a great sign of will power and loyalty to Hitler, their former leader, that most of the imprisoned Nazis stuck to their agreed suicide story, despite the tortures and deprivations in Russian prisons. That some of them broke under torture and admitted to the fake suicide story (as the Russians reported) is also not surprising.

More about the interrogation of the captured German bunker survivors is shown in a recently available book, translated from a secret Russian dossier[13].

It states that the prisoners Linge and Bauer were transferred in February of 1946 from the Lubyianka prison in Moscow to the custody of the NKVD. They were kept strictly apart and were given an informer as a cellmate. The purpose of this procedure was to clear up the previous statements that produced so many contradictions about the circumstances of Hitler's death.

It is striking that the NKVD made no attempt to contact their rival intelligence services, namely SMERSH and GRU, in order to compare information, perhaps from other prisoners.

The NKVD interrogations, starting in the middle of February 1946, included the usual methods, such as torture, sleep deprivation, food deprivation and threats against families. Bauer, with his severely wounded legs, said to his fellow inmate, "When I think that I will be tortured, I now regret that I did not commit suicide." Sure enough, he was beaten shortly thereafter by an interrogation officer.

Surprisingly, the interrogators were not interested in important military questions such as the German rockets, or the German atomic bomb project, but dwelt instead on such matters as agents' reports that Hitler may have international friends in Argentina.[13] This again indicates that the Russians might have known that Hitler traveled to Argentina.

As a result of the contradictory information obtained from the prisoner and from the insufficient identification of the "two burned corpses", Russia maintained in the years after 1945 and till the death of Stalin in 1953, that Hitler was not dead but had fled. Note, this is in contrast to the Trevor-Roper explanation (subsequently adapted by other historians) that the "cold war" atmosphere made the Russian lie a about Hitler!

Notes

[1] Joachimsthaler, Anton, *The Last Days Of Hitler*, Cassell & Co., London, 1995. *Der S*

[2] Martin Bormann was this mole, according to Louis Kilzer in—*Der Spiegel, a* German news magzine, No. 14, 1992, p. 110.

3 *THE HITLER BOOK*, The secret dossier prepared for Stalin from the interrogations of Hitler's personal aides. PUBLIC AFFAIRS, New York, 2005,

[4] From the summary report of the Russian Army investigation into the disappearance of Hitler, dated May 1946. See also "A Viking Funeral" chapter.

5.Joachimsthaler, Anton, The Last Days Of Hitler, Casell & Co. London, 1995.

6.Moscow.

[7] Joachimsthaler, Anton, *The Last Days Of Hitler*, Cassell & Co., London, 1995.

8 This is not surprising, since the Russians already knew that he was lying about the suicide.

9 For the re-enactment of the alleged cremation in the bunker garden.

[10]This was probably true prior to the double's first use after July 20, 1944. Note, that the double's domicile (Breslau) matches Müler's description.

[11 & 12]Joachimsthaler, Anton, *The Last Days Of Hitler*, Cassell & Co., London, 1995.

[13] *THE HITLER BOOK, The secret Dossier Prepared For Stalin from the Interrogations of Hitler's Personal Aides*, Public Affairs, New York, 2005, pp. 284-287.

13 | THE FATE OF EVA BRAUN

In order to fully understand the fate of the real Adolf Hitler during those last April days in 1945, we have to consider what happened to his mistress and later wife.

Eva Anna Paula Braun was born on June 12, 1912 in Munich. She attended a convent school where she apparently learned French and English, and completed business courses in 1928. She got to know Hitler in October 1929 and established a relationship with him at the end of 1930, when she worked for the photographer Heinrich Hoffmann. In 1935, Hitler bought her a small house in Bogenhausen, Bavaria. From then on she was often a guest at the Berghof, Hitler's mountain retreat, but Eva had to stay in the background on all official occasions. Her presence was practically unknown to the German public and she had contacts only with a select number of Hitler's inner circle. Incidentally, Eva Braun seems to have been a devout Catholic, since she went regularly to Sunday mass at the Berchtesgaden church, according to the local priest. Despite her faith, she tried to commit suicide at least once by shooting herself with her father's pistol. This was probably caused by frustration over Hitler's long absences and over her virtual isolation from ordinary people. Yet there must have been love and affection between the two. The wife of the janitor in Hitler's Munich apartment told the press after 1945 that "Hitler and Miss Braun were very much in love", and, "you can be sure wherever Hitler is – dead or alive – Eva is at his side."

Much has been made of Hitler's sex life, part of it by tabloid writers in the popular press after World War Two and partly by Allied propaganda during the war. There were women who claimed to have been lovers of Hitler, at varying times.[1] All these stories tend to lack credibility, especially if one considers the motivation for spreading such rumors.

Lacking information to the contrary, we have to assume that the relationship between Hitler and Eva Braun was monogamous. Just consider the time he spent at head quarters and his frequent state of exhaustion and frustration, at least during the later war years. Hitler and Braun became lovers sometime in 1932 and stayed intimate when time allowed. Later, during the final war years, Eva Braun asked Hitler's doctor, Morell, if he could not give Hitler some medication in order to strengthen his libido.[2]

Practically no one in Germany knew of Eva Braun's existence during or before the war. Even the Russian generals had no clue. For example, on May 8, 1945, Marshall Zhukov identified Eva as "Hitler's secretary" and on June 6, 1945 as "a cinema actress".

Towards the end of the war Eva Braun visited Berlin on January 19, 1945. She returned on February 2 to Munich and then went back for the last time on March 7, traveling by train to Berlin, where she stayed with Hitler till the end. There is an account by a stenographer Herrgesell, who told the Allies that he saw Hitler for the last time on April 22, and Eva Braun was with him (this is the date of her apparent departure with Hitler from Berlin).[3]

Little is known about her personality but there seems to have been love between these two quite different characters. It is understandable that she chafed under the strain of always having to stay in the background.

As described in Joachimsthaler's book:

"Eva Braun was pretty, rather than beautiful, had an attractive figure and liked all kinds of sports. In Eva Braun's company, Adolf Hitler could relax. By and large, she never betrayed his confidence and never attempted to influence him in his personal or political affairs."[4]

Hitler's housekeeper Anni Winter stated in 1948 that "Eva Braun was not very intelligent". However, we may take this statement with a pinch of salt, since Frau Winter was only in charge of Hitler's Munich apartment, while Eva Braun was in charge[5] of the "Berghof", Hitler's mountain retreat. There could have been a touch of rivalry at play. In any case, C. Schröder, one of Hitler's oldest secretaries described Eva as "very energetic and resolute."[6]

According to Nicolaus von Below, Eva Braun arrived at the bunker (actually at the Reich Chancellery) in March of 1945, very much against the will of Adolf Hitler. However she was determined to stay and lived in a room adjacent to Hitler's. Below described her as follows:

"She was always dressed carefully and tastefully, was an example to all in her conduct, and showed no sign of weakness to the very last."

In the bunker too, she apparently stayed out of the limelight but had meals together with Hitler and some of his secretaries, at least prior to April 22. (This is in contrast to the behavior of the person pretending to be Eva Braun after this date as we shall see later).

Let's now go to the days after April 21. According to O'Donnell, when the secretaries J. Wolf and C. Schröder had left on April 22nd, it was said that: at 6 p.m. "Eva Braun and Frau Goebbels arrived."[7] Where did this Eva Braun come from? Officially, the real Eva should have never left the bunker since her known arrival there on April 15.[8] Was this

"Eva Braun" another fake? This is a strong possibility, since according to the testimony of the remaining secretaries, and as reported by O'Donnell, Hitler's double refused to take his meals with what we may call the new "Eva". He also mentioned:

"...one notes here in passing, that on this evening[9] (22, April) the Fuehrer and his mistress were neither keeping the same hours nor sharing the same bed."

I assume from the fact that she arrived with Frau Goebbels, that this Eva Braun could in reality have been a member of the Goebbels' household, or one of Goebbels' trained actresses.

Here is another hint: again, from O' Donnell's book we read a statement from Dr. Schenck (also cited previously) that during his apparently first visit to the bunker on April 29, he was invited later, around 2.30 A.M.. on April 30, to a dinner and drinking party at which he was joined by "three quite good looking young women".

While two were secretaries (Junge and Krüger), he was told that the third, a well-dressed strawberry blonde, was Eva Braun. Till then he had never heard of her. He described her "as the real life of the party - like a Rhineland carnival queen". And, "She did not strike me as particularly intelligent. She was banal."[10]

This seems to be the only close description on record of what the (substitute) mistress looked like during the last bunker days.

What is striking is that Schenck describes her as a "strawberry blond", yet all of Eva Braun's photos in existence, including some small amateur color films, show her as a "brunette".

The description of her behavior and demeanor would

also seem uncharacteristic of the real Eva Braun, who by then was thirty-three years old. It also does not agree with the description of the "real", dignified Eva Braun whom von Bühlow described by saying "She was an example to us all in her conduct". We must remember that nearly everyone in the bunker, who knew her, was involved in the conspiracy. Why not extend this cover-up to his bride too?

It would have been very easy for the real Eva to slip out of the bunker prior to Hitler's famous last walk in the garden at 8:30 P.M. on the evening of April 22. Remember, the last time she was seen was shortly before 5 P.M. on April 22, when she had a short, five-minute private conversation with Hitler (perhaps he was wishing her a safe trip).

One clue to her fate may lie in a letter that was found in the bunker by Russian troops.

The letter was partly burned but was addressed by Eva Braun to her parents, stating that they might not hear from her for a long time, so please don't worry. This certainly does not read like a suicide note, but rather a farewell from a person about to go on a long voyage and who, for obvious reasons, could not communicate from her "safe haven". It appears now that this safe haven was Franco's Spain or Argentina.

It can only be hoped that the "substitute" Eva, whom Schenck described, was not murdered as well by the German Security Service, like Hitler's hapless double and the unfortunate notary, Wagner.

One should mention here that the Russians again had no positive identification of the female body that they allegedly found. Even Reidar Sognnaes while stating in 1972 that he found "excellent odontological evidence for identifying Hitler" (in reality Hitler's double) did not believe that the female corpse was that of Eva Braun.[11] If she was really poisoned, as Trevor-Roper claims, then what happened to her body? Since there was no body, her fate can only be explained by assuming that she fled with Hitler. This again supports the assumption that Hitler escaped.

Further support to this thesis is given by Marshal Sokolovsky in a statement to Cornelius Ryan, the famous writer, during the latter's visit to Moscow in 1963. The Marshal said "that there is doubt that Eva Braun's body has been found."

Finally, here we have head lines from *The New York Times* dated June 9, 1945, announcing: "Zhukov says Hitler wed actress in Berlin, may be alive in Europe". And continuing quoting Marshal Zhukov: "We found no corpse that could be Hitler" and he added "Hitler *and his bride had a good opportunity to get away from Berlin.*"[Emphasis added by this author].

In conclusion, one could state that there was no corpse of the real Eva Braun. This means she escaped from Berlin.[12]

Notes

[1] Knopp, G., *Hitler's Women*, Sutton Publishing Ltd., 2003.

[2] Ibid.

[3] McKale, Donald M., *Hitler The Survival Myth*, Cooper Square Press, 1981.

[4] Joachimsthaler, Anton, *The Last Days Of Hitler*, Cassell & Co., London, 1995.

[5] This was an un-paid position. She was supported in her task by a young couple.

[6] Christa Schröder, *Er War Mein Chef*, second edition, Georg Mü.ller Verlag, Germany, 1985.

[7] O'Donnell, James, *The Bunker*, Da Capo Press, 1978.

[8] Eva Braun stayed at her apartment at the Chancellery between March 7 and April 15, 1945.

[9] This statement refers to Albert Speer, who after midnight, still tried to see Hitler before his departure around 3 A.M.. on April23, 1945. He could not, since Hitler "fell asleep". The sleeping Fuehrer undoubtedly was the substitute, "Hitler". The real couple had left Berlin five hours earlier.

[10] O'Donnell, James, *The Bunker*, Da Capo Press, 1978.

[11] McKale, Donald M., *Hitler The Survival Myth*, Cooper Square Press, 1981

12 Baumann , Hans, *The Vanished Life of Eva Braun*, Publish America,LLP, Baltimore, .2010.

14 | WHAT HAPPENED TO GENERAL FEGELEIN?

Here is the story of another actor in the drama that was played out inside the bunker and posed yet another mystery.

Hermann Fegelein was born on October 10, 1906, in Ansbach and for a while was with the State Police in Munich. He joined the SS on October 4, 1933, and was commander of an SS riding school in 1937. During the war he advanced to be commander of an SS division in which position he served till the end of 1943. From January 1, 1944 he was Liaison Officer of the Waffen SS to Hitler. On June 6, 1944 he married Eva Braun's sister.

According to official versions, Fegelein left the bunker on April 25, 1945, was arrested on April 27, and executed during the night of April 28, 1945. Yet General Mueller[1] stated univocally to his U.S. interrogator that Fegelein flew with Hitler to Spain on April 26, 1945.

What shall we make of this? For more of the story I have to rely on O'Donnell's book,[2] and primarily on Hans Baur's testimony. While O'Donnell's chapter is entitled "The Lady Vanishes" and deals primarily with an apparent lady spy (supposedly the wife of a Hungarian diplomat) whom Fegelein was seeing. O'Donnell also describes what happened to Fegelein himself. According to this story, Fegelein drove out of Berlin on April 25, supposedly visiting Himmler at his headquarters in Hohenlychen. He then was supposed to have returned to the bunker on April 26, and then went into hiding. Here comes the bizarre part. The substitute Hitler then was supposed to need him on the 27th, and at 5 P.M. General Rattenhuber sent a posse after him. They returned empty-handed. At 11 P.M. they sent another team commanded by Colonel Högel. This time they apparently returned with Fegelein after encountering the lady spy. The prisoner was handed over to our friend SS General Müller, who promptly disappeared with him. During the night of April 27, he was supposedly brought back to the bunker and court-martialed by a tribunal consisting of Generals Burgdorf, Krebs and Mohnke. The sentence was death. Finally, Fegelein was supposed to have been executed on April 28, 1945. Joachimsthaler told an almost identical story, citing General Rattenhuber as his main source. In this book Fegelein was supposed to have driven to Fürstenberg on April 25, to visit another SS Officer, Hans Jüttner. The next day on April 26, he called several times to inquire about the military situation. Joachimsthaler surmises "that this proves he was still in Berlin."[3] As a matter of fact, he could have called from anywhere.

This is a strange story. First of all it is unlikely that Fegelein went to Hohenlychen to see Himmler on April 25. According to Walter Schellenberg, the head of Foreign Intelligence, Himmler spent April 23 and April 24 in Lübeck discussing peace terms with the Swedish Count Bernadotte.[4] Besides, Hohenlychen was about to be captured by Russian troops. Himmler's last headquarters in Wustrow (about one hour southwest of Hohenlychen) was abandoned already on April 22. The last time Schellenberg talked to Fegelein was on April 21, by telephone, while Schellenberg was visiting Himmler. It seems more likely that Fegelein went to Fürstenberg (as Joachimsthaler stated) to say goodbye to his friend and then drove south to meet the real Hitler.

Concerning the court-martial, General Mohnke (the sole survivor of this episode) later hotly denied to O'Donnell that it ever took place.[5] The other participants died shortly thereafter. Finally, there are no witnesses to the execution and as far as is known, the alleged corpse of Fegelein was never found. We also know from previous testimony that Baur was not a reliable witness and simply repeated hearsay obtained from Rattenhuber, who obviously covered up.

In his book David Irving gives a much shorter version of what happened to Fegelein.[6] He states "Hitler had hardly seen SS General Fegelein since the previous week. But on April 28, his staff began receiving erratic calls from Fegelein." At about 11.30 P.M. Fegelein was brought back into the bunker in civilian clothes and the Fuehrer ordered him summarily court-martialed and executed.

Those dates do not agree with the previous story.

Yet we still have another version. According to Fest,[7] Fegelein was picked up in civilian dress on April 27, while within the bunker new laments at steadily spreading treachery were heard. As a result "Hitler" had Fegelein subjected to a short, sharp interrogation, then shot in the chancellery by members of his bodyguard. This was supposed to have happened after 10 P.M. on April 28, 1945.

It seems that there is a strong possibility that Fegelein managed to escape as H. Müller claimed. He most likely drove to Austria, instead of to Hohenlychen, on April 25,[8] in order to join Hitler, who then departed on April 26, 1945, for Spain[9] according to Müller. His April 26 phone calls to the bunker, inquiring about the military situation, could have been placed from Hoerching airfield, and probably at the request of Hitler, who, for obvious reasons could not call himself. The whole story (and the sole source) of Fegelein's arrest, court-martial and executions came solely from statements by General Rattenhuber, one of the main conspirators in Hitler's disappearances. This was no doubt a cover story to explain away Fegelein's flight out of Berlin. That Rattenhuber was not truthful can be seen in the fact that General Mohnke (who was supposed to be a participant) vehemently denied that there ever was a Fegelein court-martial. Colonel Högel, who was supposed to have arrested Fegelein on April 28, died trying to escape from the bunker, and therefore could not testify.

There is another intriguing detail in Gregory Douglas's book. It cites a U.S. CIC report of September 1945 that one Walter Hirschfeld, a CIC agent, who was in close contact with Hans Fegelein, Hermann's father, stated that his son, Hermann Fegelein, was in contact with him and that the son told him that, "the Fuehrer and I are safe and well."[10]

Notes

[1] Douglas, Gregory, *Gestapo Chief, The 1948 Interrogation of Heinrich Müller*, James Bender Publishing, 1995.

[2] O'Donnell, James, P. *The Bunker*, Da Capo Press, 1978.

[3] Joachimsthaler, Anton, *The Last Days Of Hitler*, Cassell & Co., London, 1995.

[4] Schellenberger, Walter, *The Labyrinth*, Memoirs, Da Capo Press, 2000.

[5] O'Donnell, James,P. , *The Bunker*, DA CAPO Press, 1978.

[6] Irving, David, *Hitler's War*, Avon Books, a division of Hearst Corp., 1990.

[7] Fest, Joachim C., *Hitler*, A Harvest Book. Harcourt, Inc., 1973.

[8] He could have gotten out of Berlin by car towards the west. Berlin was encircled only that afternoon.

[9] This may have been the reason for Hitler's delayed departure from Hoerching airfield.

[10] Douglas, Gregory, *Gestapo Chief*, The 1948 Interrogation of Heinrich Müller, James Bender Publishing, 1995.

15 | THE EVIL GENIUS BEHIND IT ALL

SS General Heinrich Müller, Chief of Hitler's Secret State Police, the GESTAPO, born on April 28, 1900, was the son of a minor official. He completed his primary education and learned to be an aircraft mechanic. In June of 1917, he joined the German Army and in 1918 was assigned to flight training. Müller then served on the Western Front during World War One and earned the Iron Cross and a Bavarian Medal for bravery. After the war, Müller joined the Munich police in 1919. In 1934 he joined the Gestapo in Berlin where he rose rapidly in rank till he was promoted to Lieutenant General of the Police on November 9, 1941.

He then was head of the German Secret State Police (GESTAPO), in charge of internal security, anti-terrorism and anti-espionage. As such he had a vast network of agents and informers in Germany and also in foreign countries. On top of this he had extensive facilities to listen in on telephone conversations and to open mail.

He also had a mistress, Anna Schmidt, who saw him last in Berlin on April 24, 1945, when he said goodbye to her and gave her some poison in case she wanted to kill herself.[1]

Reading about the last days in the bunker, we can see Müller as the man in the shadows. While his name pops up now and then in the narratives, he never was reported to have talked to "Hitler" after April 22, nor was he ever involved in any official discussions on matters of state during those days. Yet, if we believe his story,[2] he may have been the most important actor on the scene. Here he was busy secreting the real Hitler out of the bunker and installing a double in his place.

He may also have made arrangements for a substitute Eva Braun. In order to reinforce the appearance that the real Hitler and Eva Braun were on the scene, he may have staged the mock wedding ceremony behind closed doors witnessed only by Goebbels and Bormann (both conveniently dead) and attended by a minor magistrate whom Müller then had liquidated for his trouble half an hour later.

Then (probably on April 30,) he had Hitler's double first poisoned and then shot through the forehead on his orders.

Finally, even though he did not admit to it, there is a possibility that he also had the substitute "strawberry blond" Eva Braun done away with.

As we can see from the above activities, Müller was quite a busy beaver. On top of all of this, he planned his own survival quite early and carefully. He had access to plenty of foreign currency, bogus British pound notes, and false passports. Besides, there were a number of safe houses in foreign countries, among them Switzerland, which was most attractive, since it was within easy reach and also a neutral country.

So when everything was arranged, he walked out of the bunker on April 29, 1945, wearing the uniform of a German Air Force Major. That evening he flew out of Berlin using a street in the Tiergarten as a runway. He made use of an army spotter plane (Fieseler Storch, F 156) with an extra fuel tank and capable of taking off within fifty meters, piloted by one of his agents who had made previous secret landings in Switzerland. Their otherwise uneventful flight passed over Chemnitz and Salzburg and finally landed close to the Swiss border at around 4 AM on Sunday, April 30, 1945.

Using a hidden motorcycle with sidecar, the pair went off via foot paths across the Swiss border, having changed into civilian clothes. He finally settled in a comfortable villa located in Bern, Switzerland where he lived till 1948.

I have quoted here extensively from Gregory Douglas' book[3] containing the transcript of interrogations of Müller by American intelligence agents that took place in Switzerland between September and October 1948. These transcripts bear the designation MUB–75–96.

We have to question whether these documents are genuine, but judging by other entries dealing with a wide variety of historical happenings during World War Two which Müller discussed and whose veracity have since been confirmed from other sources (the Hitler disappearance being only a small part of the book), I tend to believe that they are genuine.[4] As such, they constitute new material of very high historical significance.

As to Müller's personality, he comes across the pages as a something less than a pleasant person. His rather macabre humor, his cynicism and his sometimes insufferable arrogance are testimony thereof. He seemed to have been a workaholic and could not stand idleness. This is probably the reason why, in September of 1948, he contacted U.S. Army Intelligence (CIC) to seek employment despite the fact the he was living in a comfortable villa in Bern, (under the assumed name "Swartzer") Switzerland, with several servants at his disposal. In his private life he was quite unhappy. One of his two children had mongoloid features that caused him to avoid social contacts with his peers.

Yet he must have had a brilliant mind, and he certainly was a careful planner and organizer. According to interrogation notes attributed to Ernst Kaltenbrunner, his former superior, "Müller had a remarkable memory and knew every person who had ever crossed his path and all events."

An example of this was the manner in which he arranged his own "official" death in order to eliminate any traces of him. His agents in Berlin made sure that an official death certificate under number 11706/45 was issued in his name, listing him as "killed in street fighting in Berlin in April of 1945". They then arranged for a grave complete with grave marker, stating: "Our loving father, Heinrich Müller, born April 28, 1900" at the Berlin-Neukölln municipal cemetery. This ruse lasted till the 1960s when rumors began circulating that he was still alive.

His grave was formally opened in September 25, 1963 and the remains of three unknown soldiers were found, but no corpse of Heinrich Müller. The exhumation was requested by the West German Nazi prosecution center in Ludwigsburg.[5] This center learned that Müller was not dead but was employed by a foreign government. However, they never found out which government it was. Finally, in 1973 the German Government issued a formal warrant for his arrest, which is still outstanding.

Another attempt at disinformation, probably in support of his alleged death, was the return in 1958 of Müller's papers, effects and decorations to Müller's family in Munich by the Information Center of the German Army (WAST). Nobody by then bothered to check the authenticity of these items.

While the German authorities had good reasons to doubt his demise, any efforts to obtain information on Müller from U.S. Government sources turned out fruitless, despite the appearance that he worked for U.S. intelligence agencies after 1948. German police watched Müller's family and former secretary closely after 1961. But this too provided no clues as to his whereabouts.[6] There even was an attempted burglary at the home of the Müller family by two Israeli agents during that time.

Continued pressure by concerned Nazi hunters during the late 1990s forced President Clinton to order the release of all classified information on former or suspected Nazi war criminals.

This lead to a formal opening and dissemination of information on Heinrich Müller by the National Archives and Records Administration on December 15, 1999. This was done under the auspices of the Nazi War Criminal Records Inter-agency Working Group established by executive Order 13110 of January 11, 1999.

The released information proved to be very meager. Here is the copy of the summary:[7]

The file relating to Heinrich Müller, containing some 135 pages, covers the period from 1945 to 1963. It also contains copies of Nazi produced documents that pre-date 1945. During World War II, Müller was the head of the Gestapo and the leading administrator in mass killing operations during the period of late 1942 to late 1944. In the files, there were reports, rumours, and allegations that he was working for the Czech, Argentine, Russian and Cuban governments. Rumours are also noted in the files that he was killed in the last days of the war, or that he killed himself and his family in 1946.

Though bare of any information within this report[8] that one might consider to be classified, the CIA made one disclaimer, stating: "The Central Intelligence Agency and its predecessors did not know Müller's whereabouts at any point after the war." This may well be true, as far as it goes. Müller himself stated that his contacts in Switzerland were with U.S. Army Intelligence instead of the OSS (the forerunner of the CIA). However, the report does contain two interesting bits of information. One is, that Adolf Eichmann, on trial in Jerusalem (after being spirited out of Argentina), stated that Müller survived the war. The second one is a statement that "files from the RSHA (Müller's office) central files vanished in 1945". This certainly confirms Müller's statement to his U.S. interrogator in 1948[9] that he was in possession of all of his secret files (on micro film which Müller had located in a secret hiding place, the original papers were destroyed by the GESTAPO). He used these files and the desire on the side of the U.S. to posses this material, relating to Russian spy networks, as a bargaining tool to avoid prosecution as a war criminal.[10] It should be remembered that this all happened when the "cold war" was heating up.

Prior to 1948 there was an active effort by the US to find and prosecute Müller. He was put on a target list on May 27, 1945 by the (OSS) Counter-intelligence War Room. In the monthly summary report of late July 1945 it was thought that his fate was still unknown, and it was thought that Müller remained in Berlin until the remains of his old Nazi staff were reorganized at Hof near Munich. In 1947 British and American authorities twice sought out Müller's former mistress Anna Schmidt for clues, but found nothing.

The "official" U.S. intelligence statements thereafter were that Müller was dead; that is, there were no more formal investigations after 1947 concerning Müller. This timeframe conveniently coincides with Müller's first contacts with U.S. agents in September 1948!

Otherwise, the released archival information deals only with the usual rumors of Müller's sightings, rumors of his death, his supposed involvement with Russian intelligence and other less important data. For example, the CIA in 1961 interviewed a defector named Goleniewski, the Deputy Chief of Polish Military Counter Intelligence, who stated that his Soviet supervisors told him that Müller was picked up by them some time after 1950 and taken to Moscow. This coincides with rumors that Müller was working for Russian Intelligence. It appears that this rumor was sown in order to throw interested parties off the trail. What possible use would the Russians have had with a man who had arrested or killed a good many of their spies, and what use would possession of his files have been on the Russian espionage network? On the other hand, with the exception of the French Resistance movement, his information on British and American spies was relatively meager. Therefore, he would have been of little use to the Russians and, if caught, he certainly would have been executed.

On the other hand, a man with a deep knowledge of not only the European Communist spy networks, but also of Communist activities within the U.S.A., would have been of extremely high value, not only to the U.S. but also to British intelligence services. I will let the reader decide on which side Müller actually wound up. According to Müller's own statements, it was he himself who planted rumors, that he, for example, worked for the Czechoslovakian Secret Service in order to hide his true whereabouts.

The CIA Report finally concluded: "that Müller likely died in early May1945". The reader may note that this is the opinion of the three authors of the CIA report, and not necessarily that of the CIA organization.

Any admission that Müller, a wanted war criminal, might have worked for the U.S. Government would certainly be extremely embarrassing. It is for this reason that any information contrary to the above "formal" statements will probably never see the light of day.

It may seem incredible to the reader, but if we can believe Müller's own diary[11], here is what happened after he was recruited by the US Army Intelligence (CIC) in

October of 1948. He established himself in Washington, DC, and lived in a house in the fashionable Georgetown district. Officially he was a contract worker for the CIA with the rank of Brigadier General of the US Army Reserve. (Hence the later denial by the CIA that Müller was an "employee" of the CIA was true). He married a Washington socialite and had contacts with the highest level of the US Government, including President Truman.

It is presumed that Muller died in 1973. After all, he was born in the year 1900. Whatever secrets he may still have had, he probably took them with him to his grave.

Postscript: Mueller was interviewed in Switzerland by James Speyer Kronthal, the CIA Section chief in Switzerland since April 21, 1947. Kronthal was a friend of Allen Dulles who was OSS Station Chief in Bern during World War II. Speyer Kronthal spoke fluent German, and worked as an Army Captain for the OSS (precursor to the CIA), under the cover name of "Wellborn II". The interrogation reports were typed by Miss Irmgard Krieger. She used to be one of Müller's former secretaries.

(Source: www.vho.org/D/ggm2/5.html)

According To H. P. Albarelli and John F. Kelly, Speyer Kronthal died on April 1, 1953 under suspicious circumstances in his home in Washington, DC.

Notes

[1] Record Group 263: Records of the Central Intelligence Agency, Records of the Directorate of Operations. Analyses of the Name File of Heinrich Mueller

[2] Douglas, Gregory, *Gestapo Chief, The 1948 Interrogation of Heinrich Müller*, James Bender Publishing, 1995.

[3] Ibid.

[4] See Appendix.

[5] Record Group 263: Records of the Central Intelligence Agency, Records of the Directorate of Operations. Analyses of the Name File of Heinrich Müller

[I] Ibid.

[7] Ibid.

[8] Ibid.

[9] Douglas, Gregory, *Gestapo Chief, The 1948 Interrogation of Heinrich Müller*, James Bender Publishing, 1995.

[10] One should note here that Gregory Douglas' book about the Müller interrogations was written already in 1995, or four years before the U.S. Archive release stating this important information.

[11] Müler, Heinrich , *MÜLLER JOURNALS, The Washington Years, Vol.* 1, R. James Bender Publishing, 1999.

16 | MYSTERIOUS SUBMARINES

Do the Andes mountain tops, often shrouded in mist and separating Argentina from Chile, hide a dark secret? Yet the sunny valleys with their lovely green meadows and the many clear mountain lakes, look quite inviting as a harbor for man who loved a very similar landscape in Berchtesgaden, part of Bavaria in Germany. One major difference is that in the foothills of the Andes only the view of distant volcanoes hints of a more exotic continent. This makes us tempted to belief the many rumors that Hitler may have chosen Argentina as the final resting place for himself and his wife following his escape from Berlin on April 22nd, 1945. but could this be true? Perhaps Stalin, the Russian leader, may have been right when he guessed Hitler could be in Argentina? Let's examine the facts.

While we have some verification that Hitler and the former Eva Braun landed in Barcelona, Spain on April 27th, 1945, their trail ended and the official facts, explaining what happened thereafter, are very likely still hidden in secret Spanish files.

At that time there were three possible ways to travel from Spain to Argentina, if this happened to be their final destination:

1. By commercial aircraft. This mode of intercontinental travel was, in 1945 still awkward and it involved some island hopping for refueling. The small number of passengers, that a plane could hold would invite too much scrutiny and would risk exposure. There would be lack of security. The plane had to land at a major airport, which would involve customs and police. All in all, a very risky way of traveling.

2. By commercial passenger ships. This would have been convenient, since such ships did indeed depart from the harbor of Barcelona. One could hide among perhaps one hundred or more passengers using a suitable disguise and false passports. This was the standard travel method for hundreds of former Nazis and their European collaborators in order to escape their fate and go to Argentina. The risk, for Hitler, was that the ship might be stopped at sea and be searched by Allied warships. Then again, there are the customs and passport control with the possibility of being discovered.

3. Travel by submarine. This is a tempting possibility, since it would involve only a loyal German crew, sworn to secrecy. The submarine, traveling mostly underwater, using a snorkel for breathing, could arrive in Argentina undetected. Additionally, the German submarine could discharge its passengers at an isolated part of the Argentine coastline, thereby avoiding harbors where customs officials might scrutinize passports.

The last choice seems to be the most likely mode of escape, from a purely logistic point of view. We might also consider that Hitler disliked traveling on the open sea. He once got seasick on his yacht, "Grille". Traveling underwater would avoid the ocean swells that a surface vessel could have been subjected to.

One should also consider a remarkable statement that was made by the head of the German Navy, Grand Admiral Doenitz, in 1944, who said: "...that the German U-Boat fleet can be proud to have built a paradise on earth for our leader (Adolf Hitler) somewhere in the world."[1]

Were German submarines available for such purpose at the end of the Second World War? The answer is definitely yes. According to the British Naval Historian James

Robert[1]there were about forty German submarine not accounted for when the war ended.

The French naval historian Leonce Peillard stated in his book *The History of the U-Boat War*, "that between April 1 and May 6th,1945, approximately sixty of the latest boats left German harbors, traveling north".

We also have proof that a total of three German submarines arrived in Argentina during the months of July and August 1945.[2,3,4,5,6]

Here is the story of the first boat, U-530, that went to Argentina. This is how *Time Magazine*, of July 23, 1945, describes the scene:

"Off the submarine base at swank Mar del Plata, fishermen trolled through the wintry, misty Argentine dawn. Out of the gray murk loomed the bulk of a big submarine. Its engines silent, it rolled gently with the waves. The fishermen noted the craft's unfamiliar lines, went right on fishing. Just before daylight, the submarine got under way, slid silently through the naval base's narrow entrance. The sub swished past a sentry, standing with his back to the sea, and blinked a surrender signal to the control tower. The German submarine, U-530, commanded by Lieut. Otto Wermouth, 25, had arrived." The date was July 10th, 1945.

According to a UP story originating from London, the arrival of U-530 created quite a stir in the Government circles of the United Kingdom and a number of Government officials thought that the Nazi Hitler actually disembarked in Argentina on June 30th, 1945 from this submarine.

U-530 was a class IXC/40 boat of 1120 tonnes displacement; it was 76.7 meters long and had a crew of between 48 and 56 men. Her max. speed, on the surface, was 21 miles per hour.

After docking the boat, Captain Otto Wermouth was the

last to abandon the submarine. He took a small suitcase with him containing the sub's battle flag. The second in command, Captain of the Navy Karl Schubert, also very young, disembarked together with fifty-four other young crew members.[9]

The crew immediately underwent interrogation by the Argentine authorities, followed later by a second round of interrogation by US officers, who had flown to Mar del Plata for this purpose. The central subject of their questions always was, "Where is Adolf Hitler, or, if any high officials of the Third Reich might have lived on board the submarine." These are very interesting questions; why would US officers inquire about Hitler's whereabouts, when "everybody knew" that Hitler committed suicide three months ago?

This is curious indeed.

Unfortunately, the story of how the submarine got from Europe to Argentina is still unknown, and the interrogation protocols of the crew are locked up in Argentine and US archives.

The boat itself later wound up in Boston, MA, and was sunk on November 1947, north-east of Cape Cod by the US Navy.[10]

Now we come to the second boat U 977.

At the outset, one would like to know, why it took more than two months from the beginning of May 1945 to travel from northern Germany, or from one of the Scandinavian harbors, to the central part of Argentina, a distance of about 7,600 miles.

The answer is given in a US report entitled, REPORT ON THE INTERROGATION OF PRISONERS FROM U-977 SURRENDERED AT MAR DEL PLATA , 17 AUGUST 1945.

The report labeled (Op-16-Z) was dated September 19, 1945 and a copy was given to the Argentine authorities.

Interviewed was the boat's commander, Lieutenant j.g. Heinz Schäffer. Submarine U 977 was a type VIIC. It had a range of 8500 miles and a top speed of 17.7 knots (20.4 miles per hour) above the surface and 7.6 knots below. It was 67 m long and displaced 769 tons. The max. crew size was fifty-two men.

According to the engineering officer, the boat had 85 metric tons of fuel when the boat left Kristiansand in southern Norway on May 2nd, 1945. When the boat surrendered in Mar del Plata they had only 5 tons of fuel left. Therefore, making this 7,644-mile trip was only possible at a slow speed. This was the main excuse given by the officers to explain why it took one-hundred days (instead of no more than thirty-four days even at low speed) to arrive in Mar del Plata in Argentina. In addition, they said, that parts of the trip had to be done submerged, at least in northern waters, for fear of airplanes, using a snorkel for air intake. One other reason stated was, that the boat took a safe route along the coast of Norway and through the Iceland passage, then turning south. On May 10th, 1945, while still along the coast of Norway, they disembarked sixteen members of the crew near Bergen. The British held these sailors later as prisoners of war.

At the beginning of July they passed the Madeira Islands, which are located only 500 miles off the coast of southern Spain.

On July 14, 1945, the boat arrived and anchored for four hours on the southwest side of Branco on the Cape Verde Islands and then proceeded, on the surface, to cross the equator on July 23 on their way to Argentina. Note, this about 3,000 mile* trip from the equator took them 9 days according to the above statement. That would average a speed of 14 miles per hour. The whole trip, at that speed, should have taken the boat only 23 days instead of the stated 100 days. This is very curios indeed.

Of special interest is the reasons given by the boat's Captain why he ignored the orders of his Commander Admiral Doenitz on May 4th, 1945, to cease all actions and return to base, and Doenitz's subsequent order to surrender the boat to the Allies[7].

Captain Schäffer's excuse for not following orders to surrender, was, that there was poor radio reception, and that he suspected that the surrender broadcasts were Allied propaganda.

This is highly suspect. He claimed that on May 10th (two days after Germany's surrender) that he gave the crew the choice to disembark in Norway or to continue on to Argentina. This is very inconsistent with the previous pretension of not knowing that Germany had capitulated. Even if he did no hear the surrender broadcasts, why did he then decide to go to Argentina, while Germany, in his opinion was still at war? The real reason for disembarking the crew might very well have been to make room for additional passengers, or cargo, that he would take on later, perhaps in Spain.

Such passengers, or cargo, could have been taken on board either off Cape Finisterre (at the most western point of Spain), in Madeira, or on the Cape Verde Islands, all lying within the stated route of U-977. The embarkation could also have taken place in Hamburg, Germany on April 30th, 1945, if we can believe a Russian intelligence report, discussed elsewhere.

During his interrogation, Captain Schäffer assured his captors that the reasons for his trip to Argentina was simply to escape and that he was not on a secret mission. Nevertheless he did not to appear be believed, since he was repeatedly asked by his captors: "Where is Hitler hiding?" an indication, that the Allies assumed, even during the summer of 1945, that Hitler escaped from Berlin![8]

He also stated that he left his Navy base in Norway under the battle cry, "We shall never capitulate. Better death than slavery." One must also remember that his crew was very young, most sailors were barely 18 years old. Schaeffer himself was only twenty-four on the day of his final departure. Such young crew tended to be very idealistic, and one may even say they were "brainwashed" by the Nazis.

Another puzzle is: why did it take the U-boat from July 23rd to August 17, 1945 (twenty-four days) to go from the equator to Mar del Plata in Argentina, a distance of less than 3,300 miles.

From the information given by the Captain, the boat averaged a speed of 11.5 miles per hour (or 10 nautical miles per hour) which equals 276 miles per day, while cruising the South Atlantic. Such a speed would place him at their point of surrender, Mar del Plata, on August 5th, 1945. Yet the boat only arrived on August 17th. There are twelve days unaccounted for. This would have given Captain Schäffer ample time to continue further south to a destination near the Gulf of San Matias, arriving there around August 8th, discharge passengers and cargo, and then head north again towards Mar del Plata, a distance of about 400 miles. That would have taken the boat only about two to three days. This still would leave six days to spare, which are again unaccounted for. Accounting for all this extra time, the boat could have easily been at the coast of Patagonia on July 28th, as is assumed.

When the crew surrendered the boat to the Argentine Navy on August 17, 1945 they were interrogated not only by Argentine officers, but also by US personnel as well (see above). The boat later went to Boston, MA, arriving there on November 13, 1945 and then, a year later was sunk by the US Navy during target practice.

The third and the most mysterious submarine yet, identified from aerial photographs was scuttled by its crew in August of 1945 at the coast of Southern Patagonia. The hull was later located, using magnetometers, at a location defined as 41° 03' 125" S, W. This places her about 110 miles north of Punta Delgada, off the coast off Caleta de Los Loros, on the north coast of the Gulf of San Matias, in the area of clandestine activities, as we shall see later. There were many sandy beaches, especially at Bahia Cheek located about nine miles from Caleta de Los Loros, which made it ideal for the crew to land there in secrecy, using inflatable rubber boats, and to disperse. For example, from reference 3, we know that a Herr Heffner was questioned by Carlos Fuentes, "Did you arrive by submarine?" He replied," Yes, close to the 45th parallel south, together with the chief of the Nazis". In the same book, there is also a Herr Wolf cited who claimed that he arrived by submarine and later lived in Bariloche. This seemed to be Heinz Wolf, who according to German Navy records, was the last captain of U-465, a type VIIC submarine, according to a notice in the website:

www.nexusmagazine.com/articles.des/sectretwar.htmt.

This boat was scuttled in August of 1945 off the coast of Argentina. This then agrees with the above finding. However, the German Government maintains that the boat was sunk either on May 2nd or on May 7th, 1943. According to this report, there were no survivors. This last fact makes the claim suspicious. How was one to know, which boat was bombed by an Allied airplane and then sunk? Further confusion arises from the two conflicting dates. It is quite likely that this boat was taken off the normal muster roll and used for clandestine actions only, in that case, there would have been no official record.

Of further interest is the statement that a Herman Klausen by chance discovered a short-wave radio in July of 1945 at the beach at Bahia Creek, close to the location of the sunken type VIIC U-boat. This Radio seemed to be used to communicate with the U-boat in order to arrange the landings.

Type VIIC is a so-called "milk cow" having a top speed of 9.2 miles per hour under water. Her displacement was 1070 tonness and she was 67.5 m long. Her range was 8,500 miles. The max. number of her crew was fifty-two. It could have been used for transporting Hitler and his wife to Argentina. Other indices speaking for such assumption are the sinking of the submarine by orders of its own captain and the subsequent under-cover dispersal of the crew within Argentina, after disbanding the sub. The sinking of the submarine, about 1,000 meters off the coast of Caleta de Los Loros, was quite likely done to hide possible evidence of clandestine activities. The German Ambassador for Argentina recently voiced an interest by the German Government to recover the submarine.

The Argentine information, that there was a wreck of a German submarine, is certainly correct. This scuttling could very well have happened, since there were a number of these boats in readiness for secret missions. There would have been no official German Navy records if a boat was on a clandestine mission.

All these secret activities by those German submarines created excitement and alerts for the Argentine Navy. While most information is still secret and locked up, there are some documents that have been made public. For example, on July 25th, 1945, the Argentine Navy reported sighting of a submarine in the area of Claromecó. Navy and air patrols were dispatched into the area in order to investigate.

Also, in a communication dated July 19th, 1945, directed

at the Argentine Secretary of State, it said: "Periscope San Antonio Este, arrange for reinforced surveillance."

Note: the town of San Antonio Este is located at the most western point of the Gulf of San Matias, close to Caleta de Los Loros where the third submarine was later scuttled.[12]

It should be noted here that Argentine sources identified the scuttled submarine as a type XXI, a very advanced "electro boat". However, this identification was made from aerial observations of the submerged hull which was partly covered with silt. Nevertheless, the possibility exists that the scuttled boat could have been an advanced type XXI. This would have been a much more secure mode of transportation for Hitler and his staff due to the greater underwater speed of 20 miles per hour and the fact that this boat could travel submerged for up to three days, thereby avoiding Allied airplanes. It had an astonishing range of 15,500 miles! In addition, this boat would have offered much more comfort to it's passengers due to its lager size (2,100 tonnes). It even featured an onboard freezer to store food. Between 1944 and 1945 there were 118 of these boats commissioned. At the end of the war there were three boats of this type missing, and it is entirely possible that one of these made it to Argentina. Only the salvage of the sunken boat in the Gulf of Matias will solve the puzzle of what kind of boat it was

Notes

1 Ritter, Thomas, *Jäger aus der Tiefe, Das Geheimnis der unbekannten U-Boote,* EFODON-SYNEESIS Nr. 2/2001.

2 Robert, James, Website Article: *"Britain's Secret War in the Antarctic".*

3 Burnside, Patrick, *El Escape De Hitler,* Grupo Editorial Planeta S.A.I.C., 2004

4 Basti, Abel, *Bariloche Nazi,, Sitios Historicos Relacionados al Nacionalsocialismo.* Second Edition, 2004.

5 GOOGLE, Website for U 530.

6 Time Magazine, *"German submarine U 530 surrendered at Mar del Plata",* July 23, 1945.

7 Doenitz, Karl, *Memoirs, Ten Years and Twenty Days,* Da Capo Press, New York, 1997.

8 Ritter, Thomas, *Jaeger aus der Tiefe, Das Geheimnis der unbekannten U-Boote,* EFODON-SYNEESIS Nr. 2/2001.

9 Burnside, Patrick, *El Escape De Hitler,* Grupo Editorial Planeta S.A.I.C., 2004, pp. 186.

10 German information website: *uboat.net.*

11 Diego Zuniiga Contreras , Article in *Las Ultimas Noticias,* Santiago de Chile, July 11, 2004.

12 Castrillón, Ernesto, G. *Buscan un submarino nazi en aguas argentines*, Diario La Nasión.

17 | THE ARGENTINE TRAIL

Based on available information, here is a likely scenario of what happened on July 28th, 1945 on the shores of southern Argentina:

It was shortly before 6 p.m. and the sky was already dark on this wintry day at the southern hemisphere of July 28th 1945, when first one, then a second gray shadow of a submarine appeared out of the evening mist that covered San Matias bay in southern Argentina. The engines of the two U-boats finally stopped when they arrived at about 500 yards from the sandy shoreline. Both boats dropped anchor and began to heave gently with the waves while members of the crew scanned the dark coast with their binoculars as if they were expecting someone on this remote part of the Argentine coast. A meeting had indeed been arranged by a short- wave radio signal from the Argentine mainland, which the wireless operators of the two boats, had received a few days earlier. The patience of the crew was soon rewarded when suddenly a signal light flashed from the darkened shoreline. The reflections of the light beams danced eerily on top of the swirling water. This message was welcome news, since it confirmed to the captains that their navigation was quite accurate and that everything was arranged as planned.

Now orders were issued to launch rubber dinghies and crew members were detailed to row the boats ashore, to first establish contact and then to offload cargo and most importantly some mysterious passengers, among them a petite woman.

Those passengers kept mostly to themselves during the

long voyage. However, there was one figure who was quite familiar to all crew members; it was Adolf Hitler, their leader. He was recognizable despite his altered appearance and different clothing. Nevertheless, all crew members were sworn to absolute secrecy and to never reveal their secret to anyone.

The cargo consisted mainly of suitcases filled with personal belongings and some heavy crates. There were whispers that these crates may contain gold bars or gold coins.

It took quite a number of trips to bring everything ashore. While the passengers waded through the surf, the crew carried the baggage a few hundred feet up to a small road where five trucks stood in waiting. Their engines and their lights were turned off in order to avoid attention. Two former German naval officers, Rudolf Walter Dettelmann and Alfred Schulz, warmly greeted the passengers ashore. They originally hailed from the former pocket battle ship *Graf Spee* which was scuttled in the River Plate in 1939. These officers since had spent the rest of the war years in Argentina.

The party then drove up to a nice coastal estate owned by a Mr. Lahusen and, after a welcome dinner on land, all settled down to sleep in the main house. The two submarines departed soon thereafter and headed to the open sea, trying to get away from the coast before dawn break, in order to avoid detection by the Argentine Navy.

The next morning may have been a surprise to Hitler when he viewed the barren, dry landscape of Patagonian, a far cry from the lush green meadows of Bavaria. However, this would change in a few weeks when he would settle within the foothill of the Andes Mountains near Bariloche.

Now let's look at what others say was supposedly happening prior to the sinking of the"electro" boat and the surrender of submarine U 977.

The following happened according to research conducted by the Argentine journalist Abel Basti[1]:

"On July 28, 1945, two former crewmen of the *Admiral Graf Spee* pocket battleship welcomed – under the greatest secrecy – two submarines from Europe. The operation would repeat itself. One of those submarines conveyed Adolf Hitler."

This was confirmed later by another statement:

"In 1950, two sailors from the Graf Spee, a German vessel sunk by its own crew on the River Plata, said that they received at least two submarines in Patagonia on July 28, 1945".

Incidentally, Mr. Basti's book entitled *Bariloche Nazi* has a subtitle reading (translated); "Included are places where Adolf Hitler and Eva Braun lived following their escape from Berlin".

Note, the Graf Spee was a German Pocket Battleship that was damaged during an engagement with two British cruisers on December 13th 1939 in the mouth of the River Plata off the coast of Argentina. Her Captain then moved the ship to the harbor of Montevideo, Uruguay, for repair (on the north side of the River Plata and across from Argentina). However, he was not allowed to stay long enough to have the repair finished. The Captain therefore decided to leave Montevideo and then on December 17, 1945 had the ship scuttled in the river Plate. He then transferred his crew to Buenos Aires in Argentina. [2]

A similar story, to the above submarine landing, was published in the French paper *Le Figaro* on September 1st 1970 and written by A. Puget. It talks of the disembarkation from a submarine on July 28th, 1945, at an unknown place in southern Patagonia. The effort was aided by three officers of the Graf Spee. After landing, a number of containers were carried to a house owned by the Lahusen Company. [3]

Puget who reputedly was a former member of the French Deuxieme Bureau (the French Secret Service) stated that some of the crates transported by the submarines were labeled "*Geheime Reichssache*" (State Secret) and were sent under the jurisdiction of Ernst Kaltenbrunner, the head of the German Security Services, or RSHA. The containers supposedly were loaded at a base in Schleswig-Holstein, North Germany. According to a copy in the possession of Simon Wiesenthal (the Nazi hunter) of old records which showed an inventory of goods held by the RSHA on March of 1945 (prior to the departure of the submarines) that listed: 50 kilo gold ingots, fifty cases containing gold objects, 2 million US dollars, 2 million Swiss francs, five cases of diamonds and other precious stones, and stamp collections worth 5 million marks.

The same source reports that a certain Juan Paulovski told Captain Manuel Monasterio that a submarine was traveling south by night, until it arrived at the main building of a large coastal estate in the final days of July 1945. An officer from the *Dresden* assisted in the landing. Note: the *Dresden* was a World War I German warship, also scuttled in southern Patagonia in 1915 (this was probably a mix-up, and he meant an officer of the *Graf Spee*).

Supporting this is a report by the Argentine Navy[4], recording that three fishermen being at a position of 39° W and 61° S, stated that: "At 6 PM on July 23rd, a gray submarine of about 70 m long navigated about 10 km off the coast and maintained a southerly course." This happened five days before the assumed disembarkation of Hitler.

Note, this location is close to Puerto Belgrano and more

than 200 miles south of Mar del Plata, indicating that whatever submarine was, it passed by Mar del Plata and sailed further south, and then likely discharged goods or persons on the beach, before turning around and surrendering later at Mar del Plata.

The given date of July 28 for the disembarkation certainly could apply to the mystery boat that later sunk itself about a week later. This date of July 28th is too late for submarine U-530, to be there, since it surrendered already on July 10th, 1945. This could have also been too early for U-977 if we believe Captain Shaeffer's statement that he crossed the equator as late as July 23rd. However, it would stand to reason, that he was willfully misleading his interrogators about the dates, if he was truly involved in clandestine activities, in order to avoid suspicion. It certainly was possible, based on his speed, to have crossed the equator already ten days earlier. This then would place him at the southern Patagonian coast on July 28 and it was quite likely that he was passing Puerto Belgrano in a southerly direction on the 23rd of July, as was reported by the Argentine Navy.

Here is some data from an US-FBI document numbered 105-410 dated: September 21, 1945 concerning a report from an informant from Argentina. It stated that, according to this informant, a first submarine landed (on the coast of Argentina) about 2-1/2 weeks after the fall of Berlin. The time was approximately 11 p.m. Several men disembarked. After about two hours, a second submarine arrived and disembarked Hitler, two women and a doctor. They were greeted by six top Argentine officials. It was claimed that the party departed using mules to transport the baggage towards the foothills of the Andes, where the party arrived the next evening. The place of landing was given as the tip of the Valdez Peninsular in the Gulf of San Matias. Hitler came without his mustache and had a long "but" *sic* on his upper lip. Additionally he was suffering from asthma and stomach ulcers.

While we do not know who this informant was, we can safely assume that his information was hearsay. For example, no submarine could have traveled over 8,000 miles in the space of two weeks. So the date is wrong. So is the story about the pack mules. There is no way to travel over 400 miles on foot to the Andes Mountains in one day. That Hitler shaved off his mustache seems logical. There were always rumors that Hitler had a sort of wart on his upper lip. This is why he always wore a mustache. Except for the timing, the other information does match what is stated before remarkably well. So there must have been at least a grain of truth in what this informant overheard, probably rumors from other sources.

Here is additional information from the book "*El Escape De Hitler*":

An ex-submariner of the Italian Navy mentioned a conversation that he had with his former college from the German Kriegsmarine, Otto Nagel, who told him of a submarine passing close to the town of Rawson, in southern Patagonia, after landing on the coast of Argentina in July of 1945. In the same book there is mentioning of a number of German crew members living in Argentina, who later claimed that they had arrived by submarines.

A communication from the sub-prefect of La Plata told of a submarine in front of San Clemente del Tuyú. The prefect of the area, Emilio Cabrera, interviewed ten witnesses who all confirmed the transit of one or more submarines on July, 18th, passing in front of the beach resort. As Jorge Camarasa stated," such sights (of submarines) finally created a collective psychosis among the people and brought about a mobilization of airplanes and motorboats." [4]

From the dates of the observations by the Argentine Navy and the subsequent dates of the surrenders and the scuttling of the third boat one can draw the conclusion that U- 977 and the mysterious, later scuttled, sub were the two boats involved in the disembarkation on July 28, 1945. The first submarine U - 530 having already surrendered on July 10th, could have been just what its crew claimed: a vessel escaping Europe or, more likely, that this boat could have been offloading an advance party.

There was communication by radio between persons on the Argentine coast and the German submarines. As a matter of fact, there is an exhibit, inside a hotel restaurant located in the Villa Union, in the Province of de La Rioja, of a radio transmitter that was used for this purpose.

After disembarking on the coast near Puerto Madryn in southern Patagonia, Hitler and his companions rested at the coastal estate owned by the Lahusen Spa Company. The owner, Dietrich Lahusen was a well-known Nazi sympathizer; he reportedly had pictures of Hitler hanging in his warehouses[5]. J. Edgar Hoover commented on an article sent to him on December 16, 1945, and written by a Johannes Steel. In it Mr. Steel commented on the Nazi infiltration of Argentina and he quoted a pro-Nazi Argentinian Gen. Basilio Pertine who stated at a meeting at the Buenos Aires German Club: "Argentina is not a country of traitors, but a harbor and refuge for its friends". The article also mentioned that a group of Germans who seemed to be former officers met at the estate of the German Lahusen Company. He considers this company a "most important Nazi spearhead in southern Argentina".

Lahusen also owned a house at a beach resort in Mar del Plata where Hitler reputedly visited in later years. Lahusen had support from the local Governor Colonel Domingo

Mercante, a faithful supporter of Juan Perón (Argentina's President, also a German sympathizer). According to Abel Basti[7], the Lahusen company was formed by Diedrich and Christina Lahusen, both natives of Bremen in Germany, who built-up a vast supply system in Argentina besides being the agents of major German shipping lines. Before 1945, the Lahusens directed a great commercial empire from their headquarters in an imposing office building in Buenos Aires. Diedrich was the President of the Lahusen Corporation for export and import, *"Carboclor S.A."* and associated businesses. Their empire also included about 220,000 acres of land in Argentina and several houses in Bariloche.

According to confirmed testimony, Hitler departed the coastal estate one week after the dropping of the atomic bomb on Hiroshima. This would date the beginning of his trip to August 13, 1945. He reportedly traveled in one of two black Ford automobiles south on National Route 1, along the western shores of the Gulf of Nuevo, and then he passed through the town of Rawson. The cars then turned west, traveling through Las Plumas and finally reached National Highway 40. They then headed north on this road along the foothills of the Andes Mountains. After passing through the town of Le Leque and going another thirty miles, the cars headed west and into higher altitudes, using a dirt road, which to this date still claims flat tires and damage to cars.

After having traveled about 400 miles from the coast, the cars finally reached their destination on the outskirts of Bariloche. There, nestled in the foothills of the Cordilleros was a typical land house, situated on a rocky hill and surrounded by green pastures and located next to a pond. This estate was quite suitable for raising sheep and cattle, in order to be self-sufficient, as far as food is concerned.[6]

According to Abel Basti,[7] this house was called "San Ramon" and was located a short distance from Bariloche. The house as it existed in 1945 was destroyed by fire in the 1980s. The German Prince von Schaumburg-Lippe had acquired the original house in 1910. Originally accessible by a small railroad, Mr. Lahusen installed a landing strip connected to the house by a trail that constituted a "bottleneck" and which allowed absolute control of access by the Germans. Rudolf Freude who was reputed to have been the head of the German espionage network in South America, during World War II, administered this house. He also was a friend of the Argentine President Juan Perón.

Hitler and Eva Braun seemed to have later transferred their residency to the land house "Invalco" in the town of La Angustora about fifty-three miles from Bariloche.

This estate was built in the typical Alpine style and is accessible from Bariloche via Route 231. This route leads directly to the Chilenian border post called Cardenal Samoré. This would allow quick and easy escape into a neighboring country, in order to avoid capture.

Bariloche before the war was a rather sleepy town, but after 1945 became a haven for dozens of Germans and German sympathizers who fled Europe in order to avoid proscecution.[7] Its advantage in those days, aside from the climate and the beautiful surroundings, was that is lies only about twenty-five miles away from the border of Chile, making it convenient for escape into another country should danger of discovery arise. Bariloche today is a more modern city catering mainly to visitors and now is one of the major Argentine tourist attractions. It is of interest here to note that according to an FBI Document, file number 381, which contained information obtained from the US Embassy in England, stating "that an OSS Agent (the OSS is a forerunner of the CIA) mentioned that Hitler is presently hiding in Argentina at a ranch registered to a Señorita Eichhorn, a German resident of a South American country and the owner of the Grand Hotel Spa situated in La Falda". La Falda is a resort town in the Cordoba Mountains, about 400 miles north west of Buenos Aires. J. Edgar Hoover, Director of the FBI, found this information very important and wrote a letter dated November 13, 1945, to the American Embassy in Buenos Aires, Argentina, stating among other things that Mrs Eichhorn contributed substantial amounts of money to Dr. Goebbels, before the war. Hoover added that she was an enthusiastic supporter of Adolf Hitler and that she was close to Hitler and even shared the same hotel during her visits to Germany.

Hoover finally concluded: "...that if Hitler should at any time get into difficulties wherein it was necessary for him to find a safe retreat, he would find such safe retreat at her hotel (La Falda) where they had already made the necessary preparations."

Why was Argentina the preferred destination for Nazis?

There are several answers. First, there was a sizable German colony, especially in southern Patagonia. The climate and the fertile soil made it a desirable place to live. There is also information that the German Government had purchased sizable land areas in Argentina prior to World War II. Secondly, the Peronist Party, which probably was very close to being a Fascist organization, was in power, and their leader Juan Perón was very friendly to Germany. There is a document dated 1966, that was made public by the CIA, under number 13321/0655672, on March 23,1972, which stated, " The former President of Argentina approved, or, established the deposit of millions of dollars in a Swiss bank account for the purported purpose of aiding fugitive

Nazis."[17] Likewise, Argentina was a center for German espionage activity in South America during World War II. It should also be noted that Argentina only reluctantly declared war on Germany, albeit quite late, in March of 1945.

There is a letter by a Herr Fuldner, a German agent, which was sent in November of 1944 to his bosses in Berlin. It states that in order to prevent difficulties for himself, he had relinquished all his German positions and obtained Argentine citizenship.

His urgent action was to preserve German business properties in Argentina from possible Allied confiscations. In this effort he was aided by high Argentinian officials, including his "friend", Perón (the argentine President). In one of his schemes he transferred a number of shares in given German owned companies to his Argentinian friends, to make it appear that the company was owned by Argentinians, even though, the real control over the assets would remain in German hands. This letter was then sent in code to Germany after it was approved by someone who appears to be the German ambassador. Of historical significance is an additional sentence in this letter stating that President Perón was skeptical about a separate peace between Germany and the Western Allies, indicating that he was approached in order to be a mediator.

What happened to Hitler while he was in Argentina? This question is still very much shrouded in secrecy. There were the usual, but uncorroborated, sightings of Hitler. For example, in February of 1948, there was a photo published on the cover of the Argentine magazine *Ahora*, entitled (as translated): "It is Hitler in Argentina". The story was told that a person had photographed Hitler at the National Park in Los Alerces, near Lake Futalaufquen (about seventy miles east of Bariloche). Unfortunately, the photo turned out quite dark, due to shade from trees. This made a positive identification impossible.[20] There is also the testimony of Dr. Del Dosco, stating, that his father saw Hitler passing through Rio Turbido, in the Province of Santa Cruz. This happened in the year 1950.[10]

In August or September of 1954, Hitler was seen together with the former leader of Croatia, Anton Pavelič, on the outskirts of Mar del Plata.

There is the story of an old carpenter who saw Hitler in Mar del Plata. However, the house where Hitler stayed is now torn down due to an urban renewal project. This house was located within the city's beach resort. The aforementioned Dietrich Lahusen, who, incidentally, died in 1962, was the owner of this house.

Some people in Mar del Plata remembered, with apprehension, a news report that appeared in those days in a local paper, citing a German man who reportedly had seen Hitler there. This man was found dead, a few days later, on the beach of the same resort.[11]

A similar fate befell an Israeli Agent with the name of Nora Eldoc. According to Abel Basti, this MOSSAD agent was investigating the whereabouts of the infamous Doctor Mengele when she was found dead in the Cerro Lopez mountains near Bariloche in March of 1960. A later investigation by the Argentine State Security Service (SIDE) stated that the cause of death was either an accident, or an assassination.[7]

Then there were typical notes made by either the FBI or the CIA. None of these agencies seemed to be very interested to conduct a thorough investigation concerning rumors of

Hitler's whereabouts.

For example, among the FBI reports, there is one dated February 17th, 1955, under file number 245. It referred to a CIA memo that was sent to the bureau stating,"Information regarding the subject of the possibility that Hitler was living in Buenos Aires during the approximately four to five previous years; this question needs to be investigated further using possibly interrogation of subjects. This information seems to be in contrast to previous interviews with other subjects regarding Hitler's stay in South America".[12]

Another letter addressed to the FBI on June 5th, 1947, from a US agency on the subject of "Adolph (sic) Hitler and Eva Braun, INFORMATION CONCERNING."

This report stated that this agency got information from a former member of the French Resistance stating that this informant saw Hitler and Eva Braun sitting at a table in the town of Casino (actually spelled: Cassino) near Rio Grande , Brazil (close to the border of Uruguay). While the interviewer thought this story to be "fantastic", he quoted someone else: "(deleted) who (deleted) flew in and out of Berlin during the war, was of the opinion that there was no legal evidence of the death of HITLER and EVA BRAUN and that the story was entirely possible".

The French informer described Hitler as having the same general build and age; that he was clean-shaven, and had a very short German crew haircut. When the informant told a companion of this discovery, he was told not to mention this on the outside, or his life would be in danger.

According to Mr Burnside[13], there was the story of Felisa Alsina, who apparently was a servant of the Hitler couple in Argentina. She later lived with a certain Albrecht Boehme, a former German Air Force pilot, in the village of General

Roca located in the valley of Rio Negro. When, years later, she was shown a book with pictures of Hitler, she very emotionally confirmed that this was the elderly gentleman she had served.

From a facsimile that can be obtained from a website: www.hitlers-escape.com/20del6.htm, one can read a letter written by former German General Seidlitz from his home in Verden (Northern Germany) and addressed to the aforementioned Albrecht Boehme, dated June 20th, 1960. Translated from German, this letter states in part:

"Dear Mr. Boehme, thank you for your letter from Argentina and for the latest news from Argentina. General Aschenbrenner confirmed to me his trip to Buenos Aires and then to Cordóba for a meeting with our honorable and admired comrade Hitler. He further told me of the urgent meetings in various parts of the country due to the deteriorating political climate.

A few days ago, I received a correspondence from Bitzer, who told me that he settled well in Bariloche and that he met many comrades who arrived via Istanbul (all talked about how beautiful Patagonia appears to our leader). I will mail you three more packages under the code word "Doredo". He then closed with "Heil Hitler".

As explanation, former Colonel-General Walter Seidlitz was captured in Stalingrad by the Russians in 1943 and proceeded to broadcast anti-German propaganda from Moscow. Former General Aschenbrenner used to be an aid to Field Marshal Rommel.

The city of Cordóba is located about 400 miles north-west of Buenes Aires. The "deteriorating political climate" in the letter referred to, probably was the result of a government change in Argentina. Perón lost his Presidency in 1955.

During the time span between 1950 and 1960, Albrecht Boehme was very friendly with a certain Don Albrecht who, during World War One, was a pilot in the Air Force. In either July or August 1959, Don Albrecht was requested to fly a corpse to Buenos Aires. This corpse was alleged to be that of the dead Hitler.

There were rumors that the ultimate destination of the corpse was Switzerland.

Finally, one should consider the translated imprint on the cover page of Patrick Burnside's Book entitled: "*EL ESCAPE DE HITLER*":

"Can one question Hitler's suicide in Berlin in 1945?

This book shows a different version of history, it contradicts the well-known versions of his life. The facts, which are presented here, fill in the gaps formerly not accounted for. The actions of such well known people such as Canaries, Evita y Perón and others remain in question, since documents about them are still classified, and it is realized that information gleaned from their biographies are of questionable value.

The history of Hitler's suicide rests solely on the contradictory testimony of three SS men, who stated they had seen his corpse.

But there are witnesses in Argentine quarters, who claim to have seen him between the years 1945 and 1957. These persons still do not accept the established history of the end of Hitler, even today."

The question still remains, could all of this be true? Did Stalin knew something, when he told the Allied leaders in July of 1945 that Hitler probably went to Spain or Argentina?

The notion that Hitler escaped to, and died peacefully in Argentina, sounds far-fetched indeed. Yet consider these impressive arguments:

HITLER'S ESCAPE

1. Why did three German submarines suddenly appear, almost three months after the war ended, and surfaced in the same general area, despite the fact that Argentina has a 1200 mile coastline? No other submarine surrendered in any other part of South America.

2. The Bariloche area, Hitler's apparent refuge, was known to harbor dozens of fugitive Nazi war criminals and collaborators. It has a landscape and climate close to that of Bavaria, and it lies only about twenty-five miles from the Chilean border.

3. Consider the persistent questioning of the German U boat crews by US interrogators about Hitler's whereabouts.

4. The numerous sightings of Hitler in Argentina.

5. The information given to General Fegelein's father that his son and Hitler were alive and well in Argentina.

Are these all coincidences? I will let the reader decide.

Notes

1Corrales, Scott, *Hitler Died in 1960*, rense.com, 7-13-2004.

2 Pope, Dudley, *The Battle of the River Plata*, McBooks, Press, Inc. New York, 1956

3 Burnside, Patrick, *El Escape De Hitler*, Grupo Editorial Planeta, S.A.I.C. 2004. p.430.

4 Camarasa, Jorge, ODESSA AL SUR, p. 73.

4 Castrillón, Ernesto, G. *Buscan un submarino nazi en aguas argentines*, Diario La Natión

5 Burnside, Patrick, *El Escape De Hitler*, Grupo Editorial Planeta, S.A.I.C. 2004, p. 593.

6 Ibid, p. 450.

7. Basti, Abel, BARLIOCHE NAZI, Sitos Historicos Relacionados Al Nationalsocialismo, Second Edition, 2004.

7 Goni, Uki, *The Real Odessa*, Granta Books, London, 2002.

8 Burnside, Patrick, *El Escape De Hitler*, Grupo Editorial Planeta, S.A.I.C. 2004. p. 505.

9 Ibid. p. 593.

10 Ibid. p. 598.

11 Ibid., p. 614.

12 Ibid., ,p. 679.

13 Ibid., ,pp. 624-625.

18 | WHAT SHOULD WE MAKE OF ALL THIS?

While the reader may decide what is true or false in this story, here are my own thoughts of what really happened between April 20th, and May 2nd, 1945.

My conclusion is that the "historical truth" about Hitler's death is based on an elaborate hoax, concocted by some of Hitler's close associates and members of his security services. This was aided by an inadvertent cover-up and the ineptitude of the U.S. and British Security Services. It is finally supported by the unwillingness of the Western Allies to believe Stalin. What seems to be true is that both Hitler and Eva Braun (and probably Hermann Fegelein) escaped from Berlin and either reached Spain by plane, and/or they departed Europe by submarine for Argentina.

While the previous "historical" evidence leaves a lot of questions and is full of contradictions, we now have Müller's statements[1] which tend to fill in neatly many of the holes in this story and which provide us with convincing arguments that Hitler and his wife left Berlin on the evening of April 22nd, 1945.

We know that the US Nordon Report, the report of the Russian investigation commission (May 1946) and Müller's interrogation report, and reputable historians all deny that two partly-cremated bodies of either Hitler or Braun were ever found. It is therefore quite possible that this was evidence invented later by the Russian Military Intelligence Service (SMERSH) (only published in 1968), in order to cover up the fact that Hitler and Eva Braun had escaped from under their noses, after having discovered the true identity of Hitler's double.

The Russian prisoners (Baur, Linge, Guensche and Rattenhuber) having found out that the Russians discovered that Hitler's double was a fake, later corroborated the suicide story to the Western intelligence services, once they were released from Russian prisons. It was convenient that this suicide tale also coincided with the Western Allies' own, agreed upon, cover story to explain the disappearance of Hitler. One may ask at this point, why did the Nazis not cremate the corpse of Hitler's double? The idea, of course, was to make the world believe that Hitler was indeed dead. However, there needed to be a back-up plan in case the Russians should discover the true identity of the double (which they did). This then lead to the story of the double suicide, with the corpses burnt to ashes (a physical impossibility), explaining why no remains were found. One should also remember that all these witnesses were afraid of later prosecution for the murder of Hitler's double. The suicide story, once accepted, would tend to eliminate this possibility.

Note that these prisoners were only released after 1953, that is, after the death of the Russian dictator, Joseph Stalin. Stalin himself was convinced that Hitler escaped from Berlin, even though he had no absolute proof of his whereabouts. Releasing the prisoners with the suicide story while Stalin was still alive would have been politically "incorrect", to say the least. The same reason applies to the book by Lev Bezemensky[2] supporting a suicide story albeit in a different version than the one told by Trevor-Roper. This Russian version was only published in 1968, long after Stalin's death.

We have to realize that a very interesting power struggle went on between the victorious Russian generals, who wanted closure in the Hitler affair and who were understandably embarrassed by his escape, and their boss Marshal Stalin, who apparently knew better. This desire for closure led the Russian generals early on to announce that they had found Hitler's body (even if it turned out to be only that of his double). But they were rebuked by Stalin, who ordered them to admit that Hitler had indeed disappeared.

This struggle was only resolved in the generals' favor well after Stalin's death in 1953, through the release of the clumsy, and widely discredited, autopsy report shown in Bezemensky's book. While the Russian military never could show conclusive proof that Hitler committed suicide in the bunker, they got at least full support from the Western press and from a multitude of history writers. The honor of the Russian generals was restored, at least through the eyes of Russian history books.

Coming back to the German prisoners; first, they would have gladly supported the Russian suicide story, since it would have fitted nicely with their own attempts to cover up Hitler's escape. The time elapsed between their Russian interrogation and their final release from prison (after which they then made their statements to U.S. and British interrogators) can explain some, but not all, of the many contradictions in the individual stories of each prisoner regarding the suicide and the "Viking Funeral". As for Kempka,[3] the only important eyewitness who was available to the Western Powers and to Trevor-Roper in 1945, we know, that he told his U.S. and British interrogators anything "they wanted to hear". And they certainly wanted to hear that Hitler committed suicide!

Such a story was the perfect way to contradict the apparent fact that Hitler escaped from Berlin. There was only one problem, no identifiable body of Hitler was found. To get around this difficulty it was then suggested that a corpse was found but burned. Again, why not include a female burned body too, since by now everybody knew that Eva Braun was in the bunker? Yet this fact was ignored. The second problem was how to link the burnt and unrecognizable corpses to Adolf Hitler and Eva Braun. One solution for the Russians was to use the, (later partly burned)[4] corpse, of the Hitler double as a prop in their clumsy autopsy effort. This meant, of course, that there had to be a funeral conducted by the bunker Nazis and an effort to burn the body. This certainly is the origin of the story of the "Viking Funeral", although, as is well known, any false testimony usually breaks down if there are too many witnesses involved. There invariably will be small but important details that will differ from one statement to another, as we have seen in this case, thereby exposing their testimony as false.

If we consider that the whole story of Hitler's and Eva Braun's suicides, with the subsequent partial burning and burial of the bodies, was an elaborate fake event supported by the Russian Military Intelligence in order to imply that Hitler died instead of escaping, then we can also understand their reluctance to invite, in 1945, independent forensic experts, and to publish exact supporting forensic evidence, such as autopsy photos, X-rays and chemical analyses reports (according to the report prepared for Stalin, the Russian Military Intelligence absolutely refused to give any information about the alleged corpses to the Western Powers, and not even to Beria the head of the Secret State Police). The reason for not doing this is now clear, there simply were no bodies of Hitler and Braun, and hence there could not have been any exact forensic reports.

It seems also clear, that the so-called dental identification has a logical explanation. The X-ray picture supposedly taken in 1944, allegedly depicting Hitler's head, is in reality a photo taken from the head of Hitler's double (note the bullet hole in his forehead, see photo). Hitler would not have survived, from November 1944 on, with such a hole in his head. This false X-ray picture later was used by the Russians to identify the dental items taken from the head of the double. No wonder they matched, as the US Dentist, doctor Reidar Sognnaes, confirmed in 1972.

We have now four independent reports insinuating that Hitler disappeared from Berlin on or about April 22, 1945:

1.   The findings of the Russian NKVD committee charged to investigate Hitler's fate, and originally chaired by Marshal Zhukov (and later by Secret Service Chief Beria) in a report issued in May 1946;[5]

2. The Nordon Report dated November 3, 1945;[6]

3. The statement by W. F. Heimlich,[7] the former Chief Intelligence Officer for the U.S. Army in Berlin;[8]

4. The testimony of SS General Heinrich Müller.[9]

Of course, to this we have to add the many pronouncements by Stalin that Hitler escaped from Berlin.[10] There seems to be substantial evidence the US Government did not believe that Hitler was dead, see the statements by US General Lucien Clay, mentioned elsewhere, the questions posed to the German U-boat crews in Argentina (see the chapter titled The Mysterious U-Boats) the Nordon Report and so on. It appears from the journals of Heinrich Müller[11] that a Colonel Boris Pash, a CIA official in 1949, was still looking for Hitler. He told Müller in strictest confidence that Allen Dulles (the Director of the CIA) knew that Hitler flew to Spain at the end of World War II. Another interesting tidbit about the search for Hitler is that, according to Müller, a group of five members of a Zionist group that was trying to find Hitler in Spain disappeared there without a trace in 1948.

There will be an effort calling the Müller interrogation transcripts a hoax, or the product of some person's imagination, especially when one considers the politically explosive nature of these writings (see Appendix).

However, even conceding this possibility, there is sufficient evidence here to form some basic and sound conclusions. The Müller statements are, so to speak, only the icing on the cake.

It should be noted here, that although General Rattenhuber and his staff of about fifty remaining bodyguards reported directly to Hitler, while the latter was in the bunker (having sworn a personal loyalty oath to him), this changed after Hitler left on April 22, 1945. Now a Lieutenant-General of the Police, Heinrich Müller, who was also head of the German Secret Police, took charge, being Rattehuber's superior officer. Müller controlled all the strings in the bunker from the evening of April 22, 1945 till the very end.

Here are the salient points confirming Hitler's escape and using nothing but the accepted statements and testimony printed and recorded in the listed references indicating what had happened, even omitting Müller's testimony:

- There was no positive identification of any Hitler corpse in Berlin, at least not one that would stand up to a thorough forensic investigation.
- There was no identified corpse found of Eva Braun nor was an autopsy conducted.

- There is no dispute that a corpse representing a Hitler double was found. This indicates a conspiracy and probably a murder. The Nazis did not cremate this corpse.

- All surviving witnesses agree to the reduced mental state, erratic behaviour, poor physical condition, short attention span, different sleeping pattern and loss of power, of the man remaining in the bunker after April 22, 1945 all very uncharacteristic of the real Hitler. This evidence points to a different person, a double.

- There was no physical evidence found from the room where the supposed double suicide happened, except some bloodstains that most likely came from the double, who was shot.

- There may have been a mock funeral of two unidentified corpses and two dogs, Iprobably arranged by Russian investigators in April of 1946 to verify the story of their prisoners. However, this does not disprove Hitler's disappearance. On the contrary, it proves that the Nazi witnesses were lying.

- The testimonies of important surviving eyewitnesses conflict which each other on the most important details.

- There was the conviction and the many statements of Stalin, indicating that Hitler did escape.

- The last photograph taken of the Fuehrer was on April 21, 1945, the day prior to his departure from Berlin. There exist no photos thereafter.

- It was confirmed by several witnesses that the person supposed to be Hitler, after April 22, could not make any important decisions on his own (these were made primarily by Goebbels, and to a lesser extend by Bormann). In addition, this

"Fuehrer" was under virtual house arrest.

- That the assumed Hitler and Eva Braun never shared the bed or dinner table after April 22, contrary to their habit prior to this date.

- According to the Nordon Report, and the Russian investigative report of May 1946, no identifiable bodies of Hitler and Eva Braun were ever found by the Russians. This was confirmed by the well-known historians Joachim Fest and Anton Joachimsthaler. It also was confirmed by the former Chief Intelligence Officer of the US ARMY, W . F. Heimlich.

- That the Russians in 1960 published a photo of the unburnt corpse of Hitler's double, stating it to be the real Hitler, contradicting their previously announced finding of a burnt corpse (see also above).

- That Hitler's will must have been pre-signed, since it appoints Dr. Goebbels as Chancellor, even though it was known that Goebbels wanted to commit suicide, which happened two days after the supposed signing of both wills.

- We know that Colonel Baumbach, who was supposed to be in charge of Hitler's plane to Spain, was in Berlin on April 21, 1945, in order to obtain a civilian flight certificate (probably needed in Spain or Argentina, he could not fly as an Air Force Officer since this would have violated Spain's neutality). He did this a day before Hitler's apparent departure from Berlin. Baumbach then disappeared for a week without a trace.

- The Russian high-level investigation commission concluded in May 1946, after a one-year investigation and after an exact re-enactment at the scene in April 1946, that the surviving eyewitnesses were lying, and that there was no cremation of Hitler and Braun.

- We know from a photo of the bunker exit, taken on May 2nd, 1945, that the whole surface around the exit was strewn with wooden planks which showed no signs of being burnt by the alleged funeral pyre, proving that there was no cremation fire near the bunker exit.

- The presumed portion of Hitler's scull was never identified and shows a bullet exit hole in the rear of the head, which is unexplainable, since most historians claim Hitler shot himself in the temple. Yet is agrees with the fact that the double was shot from the front.

- To summarize, the whole double suicide and subsequent cremation story was not based on verifiable physical evidence but on the statements of only four surviving ardent Nazis who all were lying, according to their Russian interrogators. The German court that investigated Hitler's death stated that none of the forty surviving witnesses who were interrogated ever saw Hitler's actual corpse.

When we add to this the Müller story that Hitler and Eva Braun flew out of Berlin on April 22, 1945 and that he, Müller, was the organizer, confirming the above conclusions, then we have an open and shut case ready for any jury. What will be their verdict? I will let the reader decide.

Unfortunately, the world lost a chance to judge Hitler for all the crimes that were committed in his name.

Notes

[1] Douglas, Gregory, *Gestapo Chief, The 1948 Interrogation of Heinrich Müller*, James Bender Publishing, 1995.

[2] Bezzemensky, Lev, *The Death Of Adolf Hitler*, Michael Joseph, London, 1968.

[3] Note, all events relating to the period after March 1945 where not written by Kempka but by Erich Kean, and therefore lack all historical significance. 39 Erich Kempka, *Die Letzten Tage Mit Adolf Hitler*, Verlag K. W. Schütz K. G. ,Germany, 1976.

[4] He was partly cremated by the Russian troops the day after he was found intact.

[5] Joachimsthaler, Anton, *The Last Days Of Hitler*, Cassell & Co., London, 1995

[6] Douglas, Gregory, *Gestapo Chief, The 1948 Interrogation of Heinrich Mueller*, James Bender Publishing, 1995.

[7] Heimlich wrote in the introduction of a book by Herbert Moore and James W. Barret, entitled, *Who Killed Hitler?*, (Booktab Press, New York) the following: "I was assigned to find Adolf Hitler or his body immediately after the entry of U.S. forces into Berlin. I can positively state that I found neither Hitler nor his physical remains. Despite a thorough search in the area, I was unable to discover any proof that his body had been burned, nor was I able to find persons who were eyewitnesses to Hitler's final days in the Chancellery... I can only stress the fact that I was not successful in finding reliable eye witnesses for Hitler's activities after 22 April 1945... nine days before his alleged suicide... My own personal conclusion is that as far as Hitler's fate is concerned, everything after 22 April 1945 is a mystery...".

[8] Joachimsthaler, Anton, *The Last Days Of Hitler*, Cassell & Co., London, 1995

[9] Douglas, Gregory, *Gestapo Chief, The 1948 Interrogation of Heinrich Müller*, James Bender Publishing, 1995

[10] Michael Beschloss, *Dividing The Spoils*, SImon & Schuster, Inc., 2000

[11] Müller, Heinrich, *MÜLLER JOURNALS*, The Washington Years, Vol. 1, R. James Bender Publishing, 1999. p. 77.

19 | CHRONOLOGY OF EVENTS

It might help the reader to follow the trail better by looking at the actual, or the most likely sequence of events while unburdened by too much detail:

FRIDAY, *APRIL 20, 1945*. Adolf Hitler celebrated his 56th birthday. He reviewed a group of Hitler Youth members who had received decoration for bravery (see photo). This was followed by a reception at the new Reich Chancellery involving most of his close generals and ministers.

SATURDAY, *APRIL 21*. Hitler held his last major war situation conference with his generals.

The last photograph was taken of him standing in front of Chancellery.

SUNDAY, *APRIL 22*. AFTERNOON. Hitler said goodbye to most members of his staff and ordered them, his top generals and all ministers (except Bormann and Goebbels) to leave the same day. About eighty persons departed by ten airplanes to Salzburg, in Austria. All of Hitler's private papers were burned. Hitler also relinquished all his military commands. Hitler praised Eva Braun and kissed her in front of others.

Shortly before 5 P.M. Eva Braun talked to Hitler and then seemed to have disappeared.

At 8.30 P.M. according to Müller, Hitler walked out of the garden behind the bunker and flew out of Berlin in a helicopter

HITLER'S ESCAPE

MONDAY, *APRIL 23*. At 3 A.M. in the morning Albert Speer flew out of Berlin. According to Chief Pilot Baur, there were now only about twenty persons left from the old bunker group. All security was relaxed.

TUESDAY, *APRIL 24*. SS General Müller says goodbye to his mistress in Berlin.

WEDNESDAY, *APRIL 25*. SS General Fegelein leaves the bunker. Later that day, Berlin is encircled by Russian troops.

THURSDAY, *APRIL 26*. In the evening Hitler, Eva Braun and SS General Fegelein flew to Barcelona, Spain, from Hoerching (near Linz, Austria) airfield. This is solely based on Müller's testimony.

FRIDAY, *APRIL 27*. According to Müller, Hitler's plane lands in Barcelona.

SATURDAY, *APRIL 28*. General Weidling's break-out plan was rejected by Goebbels. Hanna Reitsch and Air Force Marshal Greim flew out of Berlin after a short visit. According to the testimony of the German Air Force officer Ernst Baumgart, Hitler was flown from Magdeburg (about 65 miles west of Berlin) to Denmark for possible boarding of a German submarine. Not possible since Magdeburg was occupied by U.S. Troops.

SUNDAY, *APRIL 29*. Shortly after midnight, on this Sunday morning there was supposed to be a wedding ceremony involving Adolf Hitler and Eva Braun, behind closed doors. There are no surviving witnesses to confirm this.

General Müller claimed that the wedding certificate that was found was pre-written and pre-signed by Hitler and Eva

Braun. At 4 A.M. the same morning Hitler's political and his personal will were signed by witnesses and perhaps dated (Hitler apparently signed these papers prior to 21 April 1945). At 11 P.M. General Müller flew out of Berlin to Switzerland via spotter plane.

MONDAY APRIL 30. Final lunch for the Hitler double at 12.30 P.M. At approximately 3 P.M. Youth Leader Max Axmann arrived from his battle station in Berlin trying to see Hitler. He was told it was too late. He was later allowed to see two covered corpses. This could have been the Hitler double and the bogus Eva Braun. It appears the double had by now been shot and carried out for burial in a shallow grave. The following is of questionable veracity: at about 4 P.M. two additional corpses and those of two dogs were carried into the garden and partly cremated. No human remains were later found.

According to Russian agent's reports, Hitler and Braun could have boarded a submarine in Hamburg, Germany (this would indicated that the flight to Barcelone was false information given to Müller for security reasons).

TUESDAY. MAY 1. During the morning, Goebbels sent a telegram (also signed by Bormann) to Admiral Doenitz[1] (who was in Flensburg) that Hitler died the previous day (no cause of death was stated). At around 8.30 P.M., Dr and Mrs Goebbels walked up the stairs to the bunker garden and there committed suicide. Their bodies were burned with gasoline. After 8.45 P.M. most surviving bunker inhabitants tried to break out of encircled Berlin, but only a handful made it. At about 9 P.M. SS Captain Schwägermann burned Hitler's study, the alleged site of the double suicide, on the orders of SS General Mohnke.

WEDNESDAY, *MAY 2.* The remaining German troops in Berlin under General Weidling surrender. There was no fighting at the bunker.

In mid-morning, the first Russian troops arrived at the bunker. At 2 P.M. Russian investigators arrive and discover the burnt bodies of Dr and Mrs Goebbels in the garden.

In mid-afternoon Russians discover the body of Hitler's double and that of the bogus Martin Bormann. This "Hitler" corpse is displayed in the Chancellery (see photo).

THURSDAY, *MAY 3,* Russian soldiers are said to have discovered two more semi-cremated bodies which they then re-buried (we only have the Russian statements but no corroborating evidence).

SATURDAY, *MAY 5,* Colonel Klimenko is reported to have the two partly burnt corpses (thought to have been the Hitler couple) disinterred and sent for an autopsy. Forensic tests conducted by the Russians showed that the two persons died of cyanide poisoning (remember, Hitler supposedly shot himself).

The following timetable is of questionable veracity (See chapters 16 and 17).

*July 28 , 1945.*Two submarine disembarked Hitler and Eva Braun plus some cargo at the coast of southern Patagonian, Argentina.

August 13, 1945. The Hitler party travels to a safe house near Bariloche, in the foot hills of the Andes Mountains, near the Chilean border.

July or August 1959, Hitler died in Argentina.

Notes

[1] Doenitz, Karl, *Memoirs, Ten Years and Ten Days*, Da Capo Press, Inc., 1997, pp. 440–441.

2 Burnside, Patrick, *El Escape De Hitler*, Grupo Editorial Planeta, S.A.I.C. 2004, p.,. 672

20 | CAST OF ACTORS IN THE BUNKER DRAMA

Here is a listing of the main participants in the drama that was played out between April 23 and May 2, 1945:

ARTHUR AXMANN. Escaped May 1st,1945, Captured by U.S. Army later in 1945. After breaking out with others, he found shelter with a women friend in Berlin.

GENERAL HANS BAUR.* Wounded while trying to escape May 2, 1945, made Russian prisoner. He too joined the group that was trying to escape Berlin on May 1 but was shot in both legs, in the chest and in one arm, during the early morning of May 2. His capture, together with that of SS General Rattenhuber, was announced by the Red Army on May 6. He was then accused by the Russians of flying Hitler to Spain.

COLONEL N. VON BELOW. Escaped April 29, 1945 to western part of Germany. Arrested by the British Army in the spring of 1946, he was released on May 14, 1948.

MARTIN BORMANN.* He supposedly died on May 2, 1945. Skeleton found December 8, 1972. Bormann took part in the evening of May 1st breakout from the bunker. Arthur Axmann testified that he saw Bormann's body apparently poisoned near the Lehrter railway station at about 3.30 A.M. on May 2.

GENERAL W. BURGDOR.* Assumed to have committed suicide in bunker, probably escaped and worked for U.S. Intelligence after 1945.

GERDA CHRISTIAN. Was raped during breakout attempt on May 1 but ultimately was smuggled out of Berlin by some British soldiers.

DR JOSEPH GOEBBELS.* Committed suicide in bunker on May 1, 1945 at about 8.30 P.M. His body together with that of his wife, was cremated using gasoline in the Garden of the Reich Chancellery.

MAJOR O. GUENSCHE.* Captured by Russians May 2, 1945. He was flown to Moscow on May 9, and imprisoned there. He was interrogated and released in 1956.

PROFESSOR W. HAASE* Captured by Russians, died in prison in the fall of 1945.

WALTER HEWEL. Committed suicide May 2, 1945. He too made the breakout in the evening of May 1 but got only as far as the Schultheiss-Patzenhofer brewery. There he shot himself.

GERTRUD JUNGE. Was raped and injured during the breakout attempt of May 1. She was ultimately rescued by a Russian major who kept her in Berlin for a year.

ERICH KEMPKA.* Escaped Berlin, he was hiding in the apartment of an alleged prostitute but was later captured in West Germany by the U.S. Army on June 8, 1945. He was released in October 1947.

GENERAL H. KREBS.* Committed suicide in the bunker on May 1, 1945. Prior to killing himself, he left the bunker just after midnight on May 1 and went to see Soviet General Chuikov under a flag of truce in order to negotiate a surrender. Here he told Chuikov of "Hitler's" suicide and wanted to discuss surrender terms. No agreement was reached and Krebs returned to the bunker in the early afternoon.

HEINZ LINGE.* Captured by Russians May 2, 1945, made prisoner. Another member of the breakout group of May 1. He was convicted and sentenced to twenty-five years of hard labor, but was released in 1955.

SS GENERAL MOHNKE.* Captured and imprisoned by the Russians May 2, 1945. He led the group of escapists on the evening of May 1, but got only as far as the Schultheiss brewery. He surrendered the next day to Russian troops. On May 9, he was flown to Moscow and imprisoned. He was finally released in 1955.

SS GENERAL H. MÜLLER.* Escaped Berlin by plane for Switzerland, April 29, 1945. Declared himself to be dead. Reportedly worked for U.S. Intelligence after October 1948.

SS GENERAL RATTENHUBER.* Wounded trying to escape May 1, 1945. Russian prisoner.

GENERAL REIMANN. Captured and made prisoner of war by Russians May 2, 1945. He died in a Russian prison in 1955.

FRANZ SCHÄDLE.* Chief of Hitler's bodyguard, severely wounded, committed suicide by shooting himself in the bunker.

HERR SILLIP. (Hitler's double). Killed in the bunker probably on April 30, 1945. His body was initially displayed in the Chancellery and later cremated by Russian Intelligence Services. A picture of his corpse is the only realistic photo, of what was supposed to be "Hitler", ever published by the Russians.

COLONEL DR STUMPFEGGER.* Committed suicide May 2, 1945. He took part in the May 1 breakout. Arthur Axmann later reported that he found his body near the Lehrter railway station at approx. 3.30 A.M. on May 2. He seemed to have taken poison.

GENERAL WEIDLING. Surrendered Berlin May 2, 1945, made prisoner of war.

It is interesting to note that out of the twenty-two most important eyewitnesses, ten died (names underlined) before they could testify in the West. One disappeared.

Names with asterisks denote likely co-conspirators in the disappearance of Hitler and the subsequent murder of Hitler's double.

As a historical footnote, and reported by O'Donnell,[1] the Russians staged a filmed re-enactment in 1946 of the Russians idea of the last bunker scenes using the imprisoned Generals Mohnke, H. Baur, J. Rattenhuber, Major Guensche, Dr. Schenck, J. Hentschel and two former SS bodyguards as actors. This occurrence was actually observed by James O'Donnell. No conclusions from these re-enactments were ever reported except as stated in the aforementioned Russian investigative report of May, 1946. However one could conclude that this was a re-enactment in order to check out the different stories of the German witnesses in regards to the "Viking Funeral". It did not go too well, since shortly there -after the Russian investigation committee declared that these witnesses were lying to cover Hitler's escape.

The overall irony in all of this is that after Hitler escaped from Berlin, he tried to tell the world through his loyal followers that he had committed suicide and that his corpse was burned to ashes in order to cover his trail. In that he succeeded, thanks in great part to the help of the Western media and governments. While the Russians knew better, they too finally conceded to world opinion, albeit twenty years later.

Notes

[1] O'Donnell, James, *The Bunker*, Da Capo Press, 1978.

APPENDIX I

As the reader will notice, the testimony of SS General Heinrich Müller is by far the most revealing and can be considered politically the most explosive information, not only on Adolf Hitler's escape from Berlin, but also other matters.

One can therefore expect major efforts by some authors who staked their reputation on previously established historical assumptions of Hitler's death, to declare the whole interrogation report either a hoax or a forgery.

John Lucas (the author of a book on Churchill) recently made such an effort in an article that appeared in the Nov/Dec. issue of *American Heritage* (AN 7682532), entitled, "The Churchill-Roosevelt Forgeries".

In this article, John Lucas made attempts to prove that the wartime German intercepts of radiotelephone conversations from November 26, 1941 and others between Roosevelt and Churchill, mentioned in Müller's interrogation report, were "cleverly falsified and were forgeries".

One of Lucas's arguments was that Churchill did not call President Roosevelt "Franklin".

However, according to the well-known author, John Meacham, the two leaders always called themselves by their first names, except during official functions and meetings.[1]

The second argument is that Churchill did not employ coarse language, and he cited as witness a dear old lady who in 1941 acted as censor and who overheard the phone conversations.

While one must admire the loyalty and even more the excellent memories of this lady, the facts are otherwise. In any case, she confirmed that these secret (and never officially published or acknowledged) phone conversations existed. Incidentally, Roosevelt's son Elliott also confirmed this fact.[2] Churchill indeed was known to use salty language and could be quite foul mouthed on occasions.[3]

The next argument put forward by Lucas was that Müller, while escaping Berlin, had only minimum luggage (and therefore could not have taken all his files along). This is certainly true. However, Müller arranged to copy all his files on microfilm which he hid in Berlin (prior to his escape flight). It was presumed, that there were a total of 811 film rolls containing between 700 and 1,000 frames per roll. All were stashed in a secret hiding place. These films were retrieved from Berlin by Müller accompanied by US CIC officials, in 1948. All paper files were destroyed by the GESPAPO at the end of the war. The story of his missing (paper) office files was recently confirmed in a published CIA report.

Lucas then said that Churchill never called American anti-communists "fascists".

While this is generally true, we have to consider this remark (on November 26, 1941) in context. In his reply Roosevelt agreed, saying "Certainly, but they (quite a number of anti-communists) would do all they could to block any attempt on my part to do more than give some more money assistance to Stalin." Churchill may have been concerned about the influence of the sizable Italian-American population (potential voters). These certainly were potential fascists instead of Nazis.

Another argument put forward was that when Churchill warned Roosevelt on November 26, 1941, by telling him that the Japanese would attack Pearl Harbor, that this could not possibly been true. He stated as proof that Churchill would not have said that the Japanese fleet would be sailing to the *east.*

The facts are that the Japanese Fleet did indeed set sail on November 27, and then headed east with the aim of attacking Pearl Harbor in Hawaii. The fleet only turned south and towards Hawaii on December 6, 1941. The actual attack then occurred on December 7th.

Note the accuracy of Churchill's warning. When he made his warning on November 26, it was already November 27 in Japan.[4]

Finally, Lucas cites that German Army transcripts of the intercepts did not mention Mussolini by name (referring to a phone conversation in 1943 shortly after Mussolini was arrested in Italy on orders of the King). This is strange since those German intercepts were so secret that only Hitler and perhaps Himmler (Müller's boss), had a copy. It is likely that this so-called German Army copy was a poor translation, or a fake document. In any case the book by G. Douglas[5] makes no reference to any "Army Transcript" and indicates that Mussolini was certainly named in the conversations between Churchill and Roosevelt.

On must remember, that these intercepts (incidentally made with the aid of an U.S. decoding machine sold by AT&T to Germany prior to the war) were so frank and confidential that neither Roosevelt nor Churchill kept a written record of their conversations. Thus we have no way to prove or disprove the correctness of these intercepts. Nevertheless, we know that these phone conversations occurred and that the Germans intercepted them starting on September 1, 1941.[6]

It is also of interest that the Nazis broke the Bern (Switzerland)/Washington code according to an interrogation statement made by the head of the German Foreign Intelligence Service, Walter Schellenberg to his American OSS interrogators.[7]

One can conclude that Mr. Lucas's arguments to prove that the intercept were forgeries were ill researched and are spurious.

Notes

[1] Meacham, John, *Franklin and Winston*, Random House, Inc., 2003.

[2] Roosevelt, Elliott, *As He Saw It*, Duell, Sloan and Pearce, New York, 1946.

[3] Cannadine, David, *In Churchill's Shadow*, Oxford University Press, 2003, pp. 57–58.

[4] Weill, Susan, *Pearl Harbor*, Tehabi Books, Inc., 2000.

[5] Douglas, Gregory, *Gestapo Chief, The 1948 Interrogation of Heinrich Müller*, James Bender Publishing, 1995

[6] Irvine, David, *Hitler's War*, the Viking Press, New York, 1977, p. 419

7 Thomas, Hugh, The Strange Death Of Heinrich Himmler, St. Martin's Press, New York, 2002, p.. 235.

APPENDIX II

COMMENTS ON THE RECENTLY RELEASED BOOK ENTITLED: *HITLER'S DEATH – RUSSIA'S LAST GREAT SECRETS FROM THE FILES OF THE KGB.* (Chaucer Press 2005).

This book, with a somewhat miss-leading title, contains translated selected files, documents, interrogation reports and photographs on the subject of Hitler's alleged death in April of 1945.

Most of the interrogation reports reveal little that is not already published. Some of the answers, attributed to the German prisoners, seem to be "politically edited". In other words, certain phrases were added to the actual statements apparently in order to please the political expectations of their superiors.

For example, in the interrogation report of Hanna Reitch, the flyer who visited the bunker between April 26 and April 27, 1945; she was quoted to have stated that, "Hitler finished his life as a criminal in the eyes of the world", yet the interrogator added that "Hitler was criminally incapable". (pages 213 and 220).

Of interest is Ms. Reitch's statement that she originally planned to fly by Helicopter to Berlin (the method Hitler was supposed to have used to escape).

All in all some of her statements seem not to the liking of her interrogator, since he remarked, "her information can not be considered absolutely accurate", and "every time she uses the word honor, she gives the wrong information".

The most interesting, and new, information was contained in the interrogation report about Hans Rattenhuber, Chief of Hitler's bodyguards. He quoted to say (on page 195) that "Linge shot Hitler". This statement certainly contradicts the suicide theory and it exposes the lies of the so-called eye witnesses.

As to the appearance of the so-called Hitler (see chapter 4), we can read the testimony of General Weidling, the last Commander of Berlin. On page 225 Weidling stated that he met "Hitler" on April 23 in the bunker, were he was greeted by a weak man who was barely able to rise and who had to support himself with both hands on the table. His face was puffy and his eyes were feverish bright. This Hitler asked Weidling: "Have we met before?" to which the General replied: "Yes, two years ago when you gave me a medal". It is understandable that the "double" was not able to remember this (the real Hitler had an excellent memory).

One must remember, while reading these reports, that these interrogations were conducted by SMERSH, the Russian Army Intelligence Service, who tried to prove that Hitler committed suicide thereby convincing Stalin that Hitler did not escape from Berlin. Alas, this did not work.

On page 93 we find an autopsy report on the dog, previously poisoned by Sergeant Tarnow in order to test the cyanide. It stated that the dog's pelt was gray. This proves that it was not Hitler's dog since that one had a brown pelt. Hitler reportedly took his dog Blondi with him when he left Berlin.

There are some interesting photographs in the book. On page 111 there is shown an open wooden box containing an unrecognizable black mass, purportedly showing the corpse of Adolf Hitler (most likely the incinerated corpse of the double). On page 114 and 115 we are shown the presumed scull of Hitler with the un-explained bullet hole at the rear of the cranium. Finally, on page 29 and page 80 there are photos of the rear bunker exit with the spot of the alleged cremation marked by an X (the spot was covered by a bundle of wooden planks, none burned).

The most astonishing part of the book is that it took seven witnesses ranging from a German Admiral to the Chancellery cook, all duly recorded and notarized, to identify the badly burned corpses of Dr J. Goebbels and his wife. Yet there was not one single witness requested to identify the alleged corpses of Adolf Hitler and Eva Hitler-Braun. The obvious conclusion, shared by historians, is that there were no such corpses.

BIBLIOGRAPHY

American Heritage, *Pictorial History Of World War II*, Heritage Publishing Co. Inc., 1966, p. 574.

Barnett, Correlli, *The Collapse Of British Power*, Sutton Publishing Ltd., 1997, p. 591.

Baumann, Hans, The *Vanished Life of Eva Braun*, Publish America LLLC, 2010.

Baumbach, Werner, *Broken Swastika*, Dorset Press, 1992

Below, Nicolaus von, *At Hitler's Side*, Greenhill Books, London, 2004

Beschloss, Michael, *Dividing The Spoils*, Simon & Schuster, Inc., 2000

—— *The Conquerors*, Simon & Schuster, 2002

Bezemensky, Lev, *The Death Of Adolf Hitler*, Michael Joseph, London, 1968

Brendon, Piers, *The Dark Valley*, Alfred A. Knopf, New York, 2000

Brown, Anthony Cave, *The Last Hero, Wild Bill Donovan*, Vintage Books, a division of Random House, 1984

Boldt, Gerhardt, *Hitler's Last Days,* Pen and Sword Books, Ltd, Barnsley, UK. 2005.

Bowen, Wayne H., *Spaniards and Nazi Germany*, University of Missouri Press, 2000.

Burnside, Patrick, *El Escape De Hitler*, Grupo Editorial Planeta, S.A.I.C. Argentina, 2004.

Castrillon, Ernesto, G. *Buscan un submarinoe nazi en aguas argentines,* Diario La Nacion, Argentina.

Chronik Der Deutschen, Chronik Verlag, Germany, 1983, p. 926.

Coates, Steve, *Helicopters Of The Third Reich*, Ian Allan Publishing, Ltd., 2002.

Dawkins, Richard, *The God Delusion*, Houghton Mifflin Company, 2006, p. 272.

Dix, J. and Calaluce, R., *Forensic Pathology*, CRC Press, LLC, 1998, p. 83.

Der Spiegel a German news magazine, No. 14, 1992, p. 110.

Doenitz, Karl, *Memoirs, Ten Years and Ten Days*, Da Capo Press, Inc., 1997, p. 440–441.

Douglas, Gregory, *Gestapo Chief, The 1948 Interrogation of Heinrich Müller*, James Bender Publishing, 1995.

Fest, Joachim C., *Hitler*, A Harvest Book, Harcourt Inc., 1973

FUEHRER CONFERENCES on NAVAL AFFAIRS, 1939-1945, Chatham Publishers, London, 1990.

Fest, Joachim, *Speer the final verdict*, Harcourt,Inc. 1999.

Fest, Joachim, Inside Hitler's Bunker, PICADOR, Farrar Strauss and Giroux, New York, 2002, pp. 116.

Goni, Uki, *The Real Odessa*, Granta Books, London, 2002

Hansig, Ron, T., Hitler's Escape, Athena Press, London, UK. 2005.

Henshall, Philip, *The Nuclear Axis, Germany, Japan and the Atomic Bomb Race*, Sutton Publishing Limited, 2000

Hitler's Death – Russia's Last Great Secret from the Files of the KGB. Chaucer Press, 2005.

Junge, Traudl, *UntilTthe Final Hour: Hitler's Last Secretary*, Arcade Publishing, 2005.

Moore, Herbert & Barrett, James, W. *Who Killed Hitler?* The Booktab Press, NY. 1947

Müller, Heinrich, Müller *Journals, the Washington years, Vol. 1.,.* James Bender Publishing. 1999.

HERMANN HISTORICA, 45th Auction Catalog for October 17–18, 2003, pp. 346–341, "Oberst Baumbach Memorabilia"

HITLER'S GENERALS, Military Conferences 1942-1945, enigma books, New York , 1962.

Irving, David, *Hitler's War*, Avon Books, a division of Hearst Corp., 1990.

Joachimsthaler, Anton, *The Last Days Of Hitler*, Cassell & Co., London. 1995

Junge, Traudl, *Until the Final Hour-Hitler's last secretary*, Arcade Publishing Co. 2003.

Kempka, Erich, *Die Letzten Tage Mit Adolf Hitler*, Verlag K. W. Schuetz K. G., Germany, 1976

—— *"Erklärungen von Herrn Erich Kempka vom 20–6–45 und Ergaenzende Erklärungen des Herrn Erich Kempka"* vom 4–7–45, given in German to the U.S. investigating officer, Harry Palmer

Kershaw, Ian, *Hitler*, W. W. Norton & Co., 2000.

Kilzer, Louis, *Hitler's Traitors*, Presido Press, Inc., 2000.

Knopp, G., *Hitler's Women*, Sutton Publishing Ltd, 2003.

Lucas, John, *The Duel*, Ticknor & Fields, Houghton Mifflin Company, 1991.

Lucas, James, *Kommandos*, Cassell & Co. 1985.

McKale, Donald M., *Hitler, The Survival Myth*, Cooper Square Press, 1981.

Mellen, Joan, *A Farewell to Justice*, Potomac Books, Inc., 2005.

Musmano, Michael, *Ten Days To Die*, second edition, McFadden Books, New York, 1962

Montefiore, Sebag, Simon, *STALIN the court of the red Tsar*, Alfred Knopf, NY. 2004.

O'Donnell, James, P. *The Bunker*, Da Capo Press, 1978

Overy, Richard, *Interrogations, The Nazis In Allied Hands, 1945*, Penguin Putnam, Inc., 2001.

Petrova, Ada and Watson, Peter, *"The Death Of Hitler"*, *Washington Post*, 7–6–03

Pope, Dudley, *The Battle of the RIVER PLATE*, McBooks, Inc. New York, 1956.

Record Group 263: Records of the Central Intelligence Agency, Records of the Directorate of Operations. Analyses of the Name File of Heinrich Müller

Schellenberger, Walter, *The Labyrinth, Memoirs*, Da Capo Press, 2000.

Schramm, Percy Ernst, *Hitler The Man and The Military Leader*, Academy Chicago Publishers, 1981

Schröder, Christa, *Er War Mein Chef*, second edition, Georg Müller Verlag, Germany, 1985 .

Sweeting, C. G., *Hitler's Squadron, The Fuehrer's Personal Aircraft and Transport Unit, 1933–1945*, Brassey's Inc., 2001.

Taylor, Blayne, *Guarding The Fuehrer*, Pictorial Histories Publishing Company, 1993, p. 242.

The Hitler Book, The secret dossier prepared for Stalin, Public Affairs, New York, 2005.

Thomas, Hugh, *The Strange Death of Heinrich Himmler,* St. Martin's Press, New York, 2001.

Toland, John, *The Last Days*, A Bantam Book/Random House, Inc., 1967.

Trevor-Roper, Hugh, *Final Entries 1945 The Diaries Of Joseph Goebbels*, G. P. Putnam's Sons, 1978

—— *Last Days Of Hitler*, third edition, *The Times*, London, 1946

Winters, Jeffry, *Served Straight Up*, Supplement of *Mechanical Engineering Magazine* (100 years of flight), ASME, Dec. 2003, p. 20.

Ziemke, Earl F., *Stalingrad To Berlin, The German Defeat in the East*, Center of Military History, U.S. Army, Washington, DC, 1968, p. 477.

CPSIA information can be obtained
at www.ICGtesting.com
Printed in the USA
BVOW09s0318131017
497364BV00001B/5/P